Pg.

Three American Radicals

Three American Radicals

John Swinton, Crusading Editor
Charles P. Steinmetz, Scientist and Socialist
William Dean Howells and the Haymarket Era

Sender Garlin

Foreword by Howard Zinn

Westview Press
Boulder • San Francisco • Oxford

Published in 1991 in the United States of America by Westview Press, Inc., 5500 Central Avenue, Boulder, Colorado 80301, and in the United Kingdom by Westview Press, 36 Lonsdale Road, Summertown, Oxford OX2 7EW

Library of Congress Cataloging-in-Publication Data
Garlin, Sender.
Three American radicals / Sender Garlin ; foreword by Howard Zinn.
p. cm.
Reprint of three works originally published by American Institute for Marxist Studies, New York; the first work published in 1976, the second in 1977, and the third in 1979. Originally published in series: Occasional papers—American Institute for Marxist Studies.
Includes bibliographical references and index.
Contents: John Swinton : crusading editor — Charles P. Steinmetz : scientist and socialist — William Dean Howells and the Haymarket Era.
ISBN 0-8133-1256-6
1. Radicals—United States—Biography. 2. Swinton, John, 1829–1901. 3. Steinmetz, Charles Proteus, 1865–1923. 4. Howells, William Dean, 1837–1920. 5. Radicalism—United States—History—19th century. I. Title
HN90.R3G27 1991
303.48′4—dc20 91-8301
CIP

Printed and bound in the United States of America

The paper used in this publication meets the requirements of the American National Standard for Permanence of Paper for Printed Library Materials Z39.48-1984.

10 9 8 7 6 5 4 3 2 1

For Martha

Contents

Neither arts, nor letters, nor science, except as they tend to make the race better, or kinder, are to be regarded as serious interests, and they cannot do this except from and through the truth.

William Dean Howells

Foreword

In the fall of 1989 I traveled to Boulder, Colorado, to give a talk at the University of Colorado. I knew that one of the chief organizers of my talk was a man named Sender Garlin, a longtime radical journalist and pamphleteer. But I was not prepared for the excitement of my encounter with him.

We met for lunch at the faculty dining room, and it lasted two hours, but it could have gone on for six, so animated was the conversation, so high the energy, so full of questions was I, so full of the history of this century was Sender Garlin. He kept saying, "It's my turn to question *you.* Equal time, you know." But I knew that we were not equals in what we had to say, and that I would have a public rostrum that evening from which to express my ideas, so I made the most of those two hours.

I am a historian, and Sender, born in the early part of the twentieth century, has lived through some of the most exciting historical moments of our time. He covered the Moscow purge trials of the 1930s for three left-wing newspapers, the only Western correspondent to be present at all of those bizarre proceedings, in which Stalin methodically disposed of his former fellow revolutionaries. In this country, Sender reported on a different kind of lynching, the trial of the Scottsboro Boys, nine black youths falsely accused of rape in Alabama during the Depression years, and sentenced to death.

Sender grew up in a working-class environment in Vermont and upstate New York. His father was a self-employed baker who, Sender says, "enlisted the services of my mother and all seven children." Reading the *Appeal to Reason* and the writings of Upton Sinclair, Sender at thirteen considered himself a Socialist: "In later years, it was Karl Marx who recruited me with his analysis of this cruel, unjust society. No one has refuted his fundamental critique." He studied with Scott Nearing and other blacklisted academics at the Rand School of Social Science, and spent several years in college and law school. He has no degrees, but his education in the world was first-class. (Apparently he found college libraries more enlightening than classroom exercises.)

Covering the bitter labor struggles of the twenties and thirties—the textile strike in Gastonia, North Carolina; the maritime and farm-workers' strikes in California (as editor of the *Western Worker*)—affected him deeply, as the Paterson silk-workers' strike moved another journalist, John Reed, and as the Kentucky miners' struggles radicalized Theodore Dreiser. Sender could never be the detached professional journalist, above the battle.

As a reporter he interviewed Dreiser, and such other diverse figures as Clarence Darrow; Emma Goldman; Lucy Parsons, widow of the Haymarket martyr Albert Parsons; Huey Long; Nadezhda Krupskaya, widow of V. I. Lenin; and Olga Knipper-Chekhova, Moscow Art Theatre star and widow of the great Russian writer Anton Chekhov. In the early thirties, Sender helped found the John Reed Club and was a founding editor of *Partisan Review*.

He has always directed his writings, with their satirical barbs, against the system: the exploitation, the racism, and the militaristic nationalism that have plagued this century, whether in the extreme form of Fascism or in more disguised forms.

The essays in this book reflect his interest in history, his fascination with personalities, and his deep commitment to a new world of peace and justice. All of his three American radicals were, in different ways and to different degrees, involved in the struggle for a better society. These essays are not only well written, but the product of impressive research. I learned a good deal from reading them.

Very few Americans, even professional historians, know of John Swinton. This is a sad commentary on our historical education: it tells us more of presidents and generals than we need to know, and not enough of radical writers, gadflies, independent journalists. Swinton belongs in all those neglected categories, and Sender Garlin makes an important contribution by bringing him onstage and telling us about his remarkable journey through the swirling events of the second half of the nineteenth century. I knew only a little about Swinton. I vaguely remembered, from reading Marx's letters, that he and Marx had met, but I did not know that he had spent so much time with the journalistic establishment (the *New York Times*, *Sun*, and *Tribune*) or that he was such a pioneer on the issue of women's rights.

More of us have heard of Charles Steinmetz, but only as a gifted electrical engineer who for many years worked for General Electric. But few know of his involvement in the Socialist Party, an aspect of his life about which GE could not have been overjoyed. (I particularly like his suggestion of a four-hour day and his proposal for Social Security—in 1915!)

William Dean Howells is one of the greatest figures of modern American literature. But most of us know little of his engagement in the political battles of his time, from his anguish over the Haymarket Affair, to his criticism of the Spanish-American War, to his role in the founding of the National Association for the Advancement of Colored People. Sender Garlin recalls the drama of Howells's life, in which he crossed paths with an extraordinary collection of individuals, among them Mark Twain, Clarence Darrow, Eugene V. Debs, Eleanor Marx, George Bernard Shaw, Paul Lawrence Dunbar, and William Morris.

I flew back from Boulder still full of my many encounters there, of which the one with Sender Garlin was surely the most memorable. On the plane I read these essays, and when I got back to Boston I wrote a letter expressing my enthusiasm. Having enjoyed them, and having learned much from them, I am sure that others will feel as I do.

Howard Zinn
Professor Emeritus of Political Science
Boston University

Preface

These biographical and historical studies, earlier published separately, are now brought together so that I may share with a new audience part of the untold history of radical America. They reveal some of the indigenous roots of this radicalism and refute the notion that radical views come from outside, not from American circumstances.

Those who benefit from the status quo, among them the media and academia, disdain to consider any fundamental criticism of the American socio-economic system. However, such criticism continues to well up in response to intolerable social conditions.

Although they emerged from disparate backgrounds, the three men discussed in this volume—John Swinton, Charles P. Steinmetz, and William Dean Howells—shared a belief in the possibility of human progress and justice. They each proclaimed in their writings and deeds the philosophy of "the greatest good for the greatest number," popularized by the early American sociologist Lester Ward. All three were affected and guided by the same intellectual and ethical influences: French utopianism, German social democracy, and American populism, nurtured by agrarian movements.

Swinton, born in Scotland, was a journalist who lived a double life: he held important posts on leading capitalist newspapers but spent his free time and personal financial resources on a labor paper, *John Swinton's Paper.* His views were never innocuous; they created tension and considerable hostility among staid journalistic colleagues.

I became interested in Swinton while still in high school, when I first encountered Upton Sinclair's anthology of social protest, *The Cry for Justice*, in the public library in my hometown, a small industrial city in the Adirondack foothills. In that stirring volume I found a mocking toast by Swinton. It is reproduced in this book.

Steinmetz, a German driven from his native land by the draconian anti-Socialist law of Bismarck, the "iron chancellor," was later hailed as a genius in his field. He worked for the General Electric Company for thirty years, while writing and speaking on behalf of progressive ideals and instituting groundbreaking reforms in public education and municipal policy in Schenectady, N.Y., in the early part of this century.

My curiosity about Steinmetz, too, began when I was a high-school student. I began to read and hear about a world-famous electrical engineer in nearby Schenectady who was at the same time a member of the city's Socialist administration, responsible for many reforms in the city's public schools.

Howells, self-taught, began as a young apprentice—a printer's devil—at his father's printshop and country weekly in Ohio. He became one of America's most popular authors, and—as editor of the *Atlantic Monthly* and contributing editor of *Harper's Monthly* and the *North American Review*—an eminent literary critic. But he risked his reputation and his career, and became the object of calumny, when he defended the Chicago "Anarchists." I had long been familiar with his novels and other literary work, but it was not until I read Henry David's classic study *The History of the Haymarket Affair* that I learned of his valiant role in the campaign to save the lives of the labor organizers who were framed on a murder charge in 1886 and sentenced to be hanged because of their fight for the eight-hour day.

Such nineteenth-century utopian experiments as Brook Farm, New Harmony, and similar ventures, together with the utopian novels of the time—*News from Nowhere* by William Morris, *Looking Backward* by Edward Bellamy, and *A Crystal Age* by W. H. Hudson—strongly affected Howells. He himself wrote two utopian novels, *A Traveler from Altruria* and *Through the Needle's Eye.* He was also deeply stirred by the Christian Socialist doctrine of social service, of which Walter Rauschenbusch of the Rochester Theological Seminary was the chief apostle.

The dramatic stories of American labor struggles and their champions are missing from conventional history texts. The official chroniclers do not describe the slave revolts, the struggle of African Americans for equal rights, the women's movement, the railroad strikes of the 1870s, the Haymarket era, the fight against child labor, the bloody 1892 Homestead steel strike in western Pennsylvania, the march on Washington led by Jacob Coxey in the hungry 1890s, the organizing of the packinghouse workers in Chicago, the 1919 steel strike led by William Z. Foster, or the periodic farm revolts.

Political and anti-labor frame-up plots were legion, such as the one against Tom Mooney and Warren K. Billings in 1916. Most historians make no mention of that case, or of the persecution of the Industrial Workers of the World (IWW) and the mass trial of 101 IWW leaders and rank-and-file members, dramatically reported by John Reed, author of

Ten Days That Shook the World (1919). The defendants were charged with discouraging recruiting for World War I, a war they saw as an imperialist conflict. Most were sentenced to long prison terms. In "The IWW in Court," published in the September 1918 issue of the *Liberator*, Reed wrote of these workers on ships and farms, in logging camps, mines, and factories: "Wherever, in the West, there is an IWW local, you will find an intellectual center—a place where men read philosophy, economics, the latest plays and novels, where art and poetry are discussed, and international politics."[1]

Unmentioned, too, is the lynching of Frank Little in Butte, Montana, by agents of the copper bosses, and of Wesley Everest in Centralia, Washington, by Legionnaires, as well as the murder of strike sympathizers in nearby Everett. Traditional historians are also silent about the Non-Partisan League in the Northwest and the Farm Federation movement in the Middle West.

Similarly muffled is the role of the Socialist Party, which elected scores of mayors, councilmen, and members of school boards; and of its press, notably the *Appeal to Reason*, which often printed special editions in the millions. These publications, while influential, did not have the resources of the corporate press, which to this day flaunts business sections but has no labor sections. The media have even created a new vocabulary to serve the interests of its class: thus, scabs have been transformed into "replacement workers."

The "muckrakers," as Theodore Roosevelt termed them, did much to call attention to social evils and to outrages against working men and women. Their exposés appeared in such mass-circulation magazines as the *Metropolitan* and *McClure's*, and in more radical periodicals like the *Masses*. Among the writers were Lincoln Steffens, John Reed, Ida

M. Tarbell, David Graham Phillips, Ray Stannard Baker, Hutchins Hapgood, Mary Heaton Vorse, and Upton Sinclair. *The Jungle*, Sinclair's harrowing tale of the Chicago stockyards, resulted in the passage, in 1906, of the Food and Drug Act, officially described as a measure "for preventing the manufacture, sale, or transportation of adulterated, misbranded, poisonous, or deleterious foods, drugs, medicines, and liquors."

Characteristic of the times is an article by George W. Alger, "The Literature of Exposure," in the August 1905 issue of the *Atlantic Monthly*, which Howells had edited thirty years earlier:

> Exposure forms the typical current literature of our daily life. They expose in countless pages the sordid and depressing rottenness of our politics; the hopeless apathy of our good citizens; the remorseless corruption of our great financiers and businessmen, who are bribing our legislatures, swindling the public with fraudulent stock schemes, adulterating our food, speculating with trust funds, combining in great monopolies to oppress and destroy small competitors. They show us our social sore spots, like the three cheerful friends of Job.[2]

In the ponderous 1,150-page *Oxford History of the American People* by Samuel Eliot Morison, one can find either nothing about such topics or only meager mention. Nor can one find the names of such champions of working people as John Swinton, Charles P. Steinmetz, Albert Parsons, Henry George, W. E. B. Du Bois, William D. ("Big Bill") Haywood or his legal defender Clarence Darrow, Joe Hill, Mary

("Mother") Jones, Elizabeth Gurley Flynn, or Emma Goldman. True, there is a seven-word reference to one of Howells's novels, *The Rise of Silas Lapham*, but there is not a whisper about his role in the Haymarket case.

As might be expected, Morison's *History* celebrates the successes of the corporate magnates (the robber barons), the generals and admirals, and the politicians. William Rainey Harper, founding president of the Rockefeller-funded University of Chicago, who served from 1891 to 1906, spoke candidly when he said, "It is all very well to sympathize with the working man, but we get our money from those on the other side, and we can't afford to offend them."

Harper made this remark during the academic storm that followed the dismissal of Scott Nearing from his position as professor of economics at the University of Pennsylvania in 1915. Nearing was prominent in the campaign against child labor, and among the university's trustees were industrialists who employed large numbers of child workers. Moreover, he had stimulated too much thinking among his students, a dangerous activity on any campus.

But where does "the other side" get "its" money? An irrefutable answer was given by Abraham Lincoln on March 2, 1864, to a visiting delegation from the newly organized Workingmen's Republican Association of New York. When told that he had been made an honorary member, Lincoln responded, "Labor is prior to, and independent of, capital. Capital is only the fruit of labor and could never have existed if labor had not first existed." Four years earlier, in Hartford, Connecticut, Lincoln had challenged Stephen A. Douglas's characterization of a shoe workers' strike in Massachusetts as a consequence of "this unfortunate sectional warfare" between the North and the South. "I thank God," he declared, "that we have a system of labor where there can be a strike. Whatever the pressure, there is a point where the workingman may stop." The following day, in New Haven, he said, "I am glad to see that a system of labor prevails in New England under which laborers can strike when they want to."[3]

The years following William Rainey Harper's words have witnessed little change. Apart from a few exceptions, our colleges and universities still do not offer their students courses in labor history, because it is not regarded as an organic part of American history. To cite just one example, the University of Colorado at Boulder, which has an enrollment of twenty-five thousand, does not provide a single course in labor history—in spite of the fact that Colorado has been the scene of bitter and bloody labor conflict, in Ludlow, Cripple Creek, Telluride, and elsewhere. Between 1890 and 1904 the Colorado state militia was called out ten times to break strikes. Virtually a lone voice, in 1953 George S. McGovern wrote his doctoral dissertation, at Northwestern University, on the Colorado coal strike of 1913–1914. With the aid of a collaborator, Leonard F. Guttridge, the work was popularized, and during McGovern's campaign for the presidency, in 1972, it was published under the title *The Great Coalfield War*.

It is my hope that these studies of John Swinton, Charles P. Steinmetz, and William Dean Howells will help in some measure to provide an authentic perspective on American radicalism and some of its champions.

Sender Garlin

Acknowledgments

I wish to thank the staffs of the Elmer Holmes Bobst Library of New York University, the New York Public Library, the Library of the New York Historical Society, the Research Library of the Schenectady County Historical Society, the Schaffer Library of Union College, the Archives of Knox College, and the Library of the University of Virginia.

I am indebted to Professor William White Howells of Harvard University, grandson of William Dean Howells, for his generous permission, on behalf of the writer's heirs, to quote from a number of letters that were for many years restricted. These letters are in the Memorabilia Room at Knox College and may not be reprinted without special permission from Dr. Howells.

Eleanor Marx's letter to William Dean Howells is here published by permission of the Houghton Manuscript Library of Harvard University.

Thanks are due to Professor Howard A. Wilson of Knox College, and to the editors of the *Journal of the Illinois State Historical Society*, who granted permission to quote from Professor Wilson's article in that publication.

I am grateful to the staff of the Tamiment Library, New York University—Dorothy Swanson, Debra Bernhardt,

Peter Filardo, Erika Gottfried, Gail Malmgreen, and Robert Eberwein—for making available *John Swinton's Paper*, on microfilm, as well as numerous other rare source materials on Swinton, Steinmetz, and Howells.

I want to thank Dr. Herbert Aptheker for his comments on earlier versions of the essays that make up this volume, which were published by the American Institute for Marxist Studies, of which he was director. I am grateful to my dear friends Gil Green, Lloyd Brown, and Steve Fuller for their constant encouragement. Professor James Kimble of the University of Colorado has been an eloquent champion of this book; for this, my heartfelt thanks. From the very beginning, my wife, Martha Millet Garlin, offered valuable insights and editorial help.

I am indebted to Sarah Nord, who word-processed the Foreword and the Preface; Kate Fallon of the Department of Photography, Tisch School of the Arts, New York University, who reproduced the three portraits; and Edward Friedman, Eugene Rodolphe, John Kesich, and Bill Russell of the Academic Computing Facility and the Courant Institute of Mathematical Sciences, New York University, who helped set the book in type, using computer-typsetting software. It was a pleasure to work with Dean Birkenkamp and Jim Fieser of Westview Press.

I am especially grateful to my daughter, Emily Garlin, whose superb editing is apparent on every page. Without her devotion to this project, *Three American Radicals* would not exist in its present form.

S.G.

John Swinton, Crusading Editor

The world owes more, far more to John Swinton than it knows or perhaps ever can know. He was one of the real heroes of American history. He lived and labored wholly for his fellow-men. He struggled bravely with all the adverse fates and forces that others might be spared the pains and privations that fell to his lot and have life richer and more abundant. Aye, he fought as heroically and unselfishly for humanity as any man who ever won the crown of martyrdom.

Eugene Victor Debs

The America of today needs to be reminded of men like John Swinton, a fighter in labor's cause as writer, editor, orator, and organizer. After his death nearly a century ago, the *New York Times* described him as "the champion of the working-men with voice and pen" and told of the many crusades he had led. Referring to *John Swinton's Paper*, the labor news-paper he had founded and edited, the *Times* commented, in a tone of self-congratulation, "He had been on the side of the masses, but his paper died for want of support by them. The very class of people that Swinton tried to benefit neglected and frequently condemned him." Evidently the *Times* sought to attribute its own duality to Swinton and thus devalue his accomplishments. For while it was well known that he had taken a leading part in labor's battles for many decades, it was equally true that he had been a prominent and highly-regarded journalist. In a tribute in the literary section of the *Times*, T. C. Evans characterized Swinton as "disputatious" and "aggressive" but added, "He lived up to high professional standards and left a name worthy of respectful and admiring remembrance."

John Swinton was born on December 12, 1829, in the town of Salton, near Edinburgh, in Haddingtonshire (now East Lothian), Scotland. When he was fourteen, his parents, Jane Currie Swinton and William Swinton, with John and his younger brother, William, emigrated to Montreal, Canada. John became a printer's apprentice on the *Montreal Witness*, and then a journeyman printer, a trade he followed until he began to work as a newspaperman. The family moved to New York City in 1849. He attended Williston Seminary in Northampton, Massachusetts, in 1853, and later he took courses at New York Medical College and studied law.

Swinton was associated with major New York newspapers for nearly a half-century, working under three famous editors: Henry J. Raymond of the *Times*, Charles A. Dana of the *Sun*, and Horace Greeley of the *Tribune*. He also contributed articles and letters to the *New York World*, the *Brooklyn Eagle*, the *Irish World*, and the *Scotsman*.

In a commemorative article that appeared on December 21, 1901, *Harper's Weekly* declared: "The life work of this stalwart, bitter champion of the laborer reads like a romance. It was one continuous battle for the rights of the lowly and oppressed. . . . A hater of sham, he fought bitterly, and with no hope of reward."

The United States, when Swinton was in his twenties, was approaching a critical point in its history that culminated in the Civil War. As a journeyman printer, Swinton traveled extensively in the South and the West. In 1856, he went to Kansas to take part in the free-soil movement, but he arrived too late to join John Brown in the struggle. He remained, however, to become manager of the *Lawrence Republican.* In South Carolina he was a compositor in the state printing office. Here he risked his life teaching black people to read and write. The gatherings took place in an underground vault.

After Swinton returned to New York in 1860, an article about medicine earned him a place on the *Times*, where he became chief editorial-writer and, during Raymond's frequent absences, managing editor. (His brother, who had joined the *Times* staff in 1858, was a Civil War correspondent; he later taught at the University of California and wrote textbooks.) From 1870 to 1875, he was a free-lance journalist; whether his writing for the *Tribune* from 1870 to 1872 was done as a staff assignment or on a free-lance basis is unclear. He worked on the *Sun* from 1875 to 1883, becoming chief of the editorial staff. From 1883 to 1887, he published his own paper. Then he free-lanced again before returning to the *Sun*, where he remained from 1892 to 1897.

Swinton lost his eyesight in 1899 but continued his writing and political work until his death in Brooklyn Heights on December 15, 1901, after a brief illness. He was survived by his wife, Orsena, to whom he had been married since 1877. Not only the powerful newspapers but the Socialist and trade-union press noted his passing. A monument erected by trade unionists marks his grave in Greenwood Cemetery.

Like the friend he so greatly admired, Walt Whitman Swinton had for years stood at his case ten hours a day, setting type for news dispatches and editorials. As a journeymar printer—like Mark Twain and William Dean Howells—he had seen much of the country, and what he witnessed of slavery, child labor, and the sweatshops in the big cities of the land stirred him to profound anger.

Through the years, Swinton reacted with indignation to the misery wrought by economic crises, in 1854, 1857, 1860, 1873, 1885, and 1894. After the Civil War had formally destroyed slavery, he perceived that "free men," black and white working people, were still unfree. And on December 1, 1888, at a commemoration of the twenty-second anniversary of John Brown's death, he told an audience at Turnverein Hall, in New York City, what the man from North Elba in the Adirondacks had meant to him:

> It needs that we recall the stupendous strength of the old Slavery establishment—its bulwarks of constitutionalism, legality, politics, mercantilism, capitalism—and ecclesiasticism; it needs that we recall the power of the interests and passions that environed it, and the subserviency or timidity of even its opponents, with few exceptions, before we can comprehend the influence of the man . . . who struck through them all, and struck to the heart.
>
> It was a new policy that John Brown brought into play against American slavery—the policy of meeting it upon its own terms, and its own field, confronting with force a system based upon force, and establishing human rights by the weapons that upheld public wrongs.

> In place of the old way of acquiescing in slavery, or compromising with it, or arguing over it, or resisting its extension, he adopted the way of assailing it by the only means that gave any hope of destroying it. John Brown's way was justified by the event—justified amid flame and smoke by Abraham Lincoln's proclamation of abolition.

It was at about this time that a writer for the *Brooklyn Daily Union* described the journalist thus: "large-framed, full-faced, healthy complexion, big brown eyes, a sandy gray moustache, bald, save a rim of gray on the outlying county of an immense cranium; a man who gives expression with rapidity of utterance and eloquence, now and then illuminating his points with a story, an allusion to history, or some passage in the classics."

In a biography of Swinton published a year after his death, his friend Robert Waters—a fellow Scotsman and printer who was the author of a book about William Cobbett—wrote that he was "above the middle height, long-haired, broad-browed, with a dark, keen, piercing eye, vehement in his denunciation of slavery and fearless in his exposition of daring views and noble aspirations."

Waters termed him "a zealous disciple of the abolitionists Phillips, Parker, and Garrison.... A great reader of anti-slavery papers and magazines, he was even then noted among his acquaintances for the impetuous ardor with which he assailed slavery. He was in full sympathy with the anti-slavery movement of that time, while most of his comrades sneered at the Negroes and made vulgar jokes about them."

Swinton's conversation, Waters recalled, "stirred me more than that of any man I had so far known. He was an ardent admirer of Carlyle, Emerson, Montaigne, and Ruskin." In 1861, Waters wrote, he went to Europe, and he did not see Swinton again until seven years later: "I came back and found Swinton one of the 'leader writers' for the *Times*, and well known in the literary and political world.... He had acquired such a command of language, such a wealth of imagery, and such knowledge of men and things, present and past, literary, political and scientific, that I thought him by far the best-informed and the most brilliant talker I had ever known."[1]

In a discussion of Waters' book about Swinton, in its December 1902 issue, the *International Socialist Review* commented: "Among the names of those who have made smooth the way for the Socialist movement in America, there are few more prominent than that of John Swinton. A man of brilliant intellect, a personal friend of Karl Marx, an able linguist, a fighter in the actual battle of labor, and one of the most prominent journalists of the United States, his was preeminently a life of action and of doing. This life is told by a friend who makes the man live before us."

Some years later, the famous Socialist and trade-union leader Eugene V. Debs wrote: "In personal appearance Swinton was tall, well-proportioned, and courtly in manner, and one recognized in him at a glance a distinguished personage. He certainly looked the man he was. His features were strikingly clear-cut, his eyes keen and piercing, though kindly, his hair snow-white, as were also his moustache and eyebrows, which set off his fine, smooth brow and pallid complexion to perfection."[2]

In *The Story of the "New York Times," 1851–1951*, Meyer Berger has written: "When the *Times* was young, it gave more space to news of science than any other New

York newspaper, and John Swinton, a *Times* editorial writer, handled most of it. For example, in the summer of 1860 he wrote, and the *Times* used, three to four columns a day on the meeting of the American Scientists' Association at Newport, Rhode Island, and he contributed editorials on science on the side."

When Charles Darwin's book *On the Origin of Species* was published in New York, in March 1860, the *Times* ran a three-and-a-half-column story that Berger attributes to Swinton. He began: "Mr. Darwin, as the fruit of a quarter-century of patient observation and experiment, throws out, in a book whose title at least by this time has become familiar to the reading public, a series of arguments and inferences so revolutionary as, if established, to necessitate a radical reconstruction of the fundamental doctrines of natural history."

Swinton recognized the potential influence of Darwin's work: "It is clear that here is one of the most important contributions ever made to philosophic science; and it is behooving on the scientists, in light of the accumulation of evidence which the author has summoned in support of his theory, to reconsider the grounds on which their present doctrine of the origin of the species is based." Berger writes, "Swinton left the *Times* after Raymond died, and science news fell off... for a half-century."[3]

Swinton's many-sided interests are also touched upon by Frank M. O'Brien, the chronicler of another New York newspaper on which Swinton played a major role. In *The Story of the "Sun," 1883–1928*, O'Brien writes: "John Swinton was among the editorial writers who contributed most to Dana's success.... Swinton, whose specialty was Central American affairs and paragraphing, was a Socialist outside the *Sun* office. He delighted to denounce the 'capitalistic *Sun*' in a speech at night and to tell Mr. Dana about it the next morning."[4]

Augustus Maverick, in *Henry J. Raymond and the New York Press*, described Swinton as "a fluent and graceful writer of great natural shrewdness and ready wit. He brought to the profession of journalism a keen and just sense of its requirements. In a greater degree than almost any other member of his profession in this country, he possesses the faculty of pointing a paragraph in such a manner that it becomes as effective as the labored essay of the didactic writer."[5]

Swinton was an activist who did not confine his political interests to the editorial sanctum. On September 6, 1883, he appeared before the U.S. Senate Committee on Labor and Education, which was holding sessions in New York City. Senator Henry W. Blair, a New Hampshire Republican who was the committee's chairman, had proposed that the panel travel to various cities to hear testimony on issues involving capital and labor. The *Times* described the event in a quaint, intimate journalistic style that is now out of fashion: "John Swinton's gold-rimmed eye glasses twitched nervously on his nose yesterday morning as he smilingly admitted to Senator Blair, of the Senate Committee on Education and Labor, that he was an editor. He said that he had been connected with the press since he was twelve years of age. As a newspaperman he had become acquainted with all sorts of questions relating to all sorts of men. He had given the subject of labor much attention and thought, and he had in mind certain measures which, if enacted into laws by Congress, would, he believed, result to the great benefit of the common people."

The *Times* correspondent reported that these measures included the revival of the graduated income tax, which had been in effect from 1863 to 1872; the establishment of national boards of health, education, and public works; the formation of a bureau to gather statistics on the eight-hour question and on working women and children; the establishment of postal banks; the enactment of laws "to prevent the holding of large tracts of land in this country by individuals or corporations"; and, finally, public ownership of the railroads, the telegraph, coal, iron, and gold mines, and oil wells.

On one occasion, presiding at a Cooper Union meeting called to protest a New York State Court of Appeals decision nullifying the prevailing wage rate, Swinton told the assemblage, "There have been more born criminals among the men of the bench than among the pirates that ever sailed the high seas." The *Times* reporter wrote, "This sally was greeted with laughter and applause." Swinton went on to say: "The bench has always been ready to sell out liberty. It supported a king in this country until the revolutionists put the bench where it came from."

Swinton's partisanship on the side of labor was no secret to his journalistic colleagues. It was the Tompkins Square unemployed demonstration in 1874 that had first brought him into full public prominence in that role. The panic of 1873 had strangled industry, and thousands of New York workers were hurled into unemployment, their families starving. On March 25, 1874, appearing before the New York State Legislature, Swinton assailed what he termed "the Tompkins Square outrage" and called on the law-makers to investigate the situation in New York City. He told them:

> In December and January the unemployed and suffering people began to feel that the municipal authorities, and more prosperous classes, must—in some way—be made aware of their actual condition, which had been so strangely misrep-

resented by more than one of the newspapers. There followed a decision to hold a mass demonstration at Tompkins Square, the mayor himself promising to address the meeting.

But now, about ten o'clock, when they were standing around peaceably, waiting for the mayor, platoons of police suddenly appeared, deployed into the square, rushed without warning whatever on the helpless and unarmed multitudes, violently assailed them with their clubs, struck at heads right and left, wounded many, and dragged off some thirty or forty, who were flung into station-houses not unlike the Black Hole of Calcutta.

Gentlemen, is not this a horrible spectacle in a civilized country and city? Do you know of anything like it in the modern experience of any other Christian region of the world?

The editorial funks and intellectual policemen have roused prejudices against these their victims by saying they were Communists, in league with the impending earthquake. Gentlemen, be not alarmed by mysterious words, and let not the epithet "Communist" stir up the same sort of hydrophobia that the epithet "Abolitionist" once did. Suppose the ideas of these people were the sort which editors and policemen call "Communistic"; does anyone suppose the thing can be scribbled out of their hearts or clubbed out of their heads?

The authorities were not quelling a riot, for there was no riot, and not a man had raised a finger when the police unexpectedly sprang to

> the assault. They were not dispersing a mob, for this was not a mob, but a peaceable gathering under regular authority, few among them being aware that the papers of that morning had published a hastily-issued prohibitory order. Only two or three of the workingmen offered even the slightest resistance to the onslaught, though it must have been hard for some of them, under the circumstances, to refrain from defending their lives. None of the victims were actually clubbed or trampled to death, but many were shockingly wounded. No charges could be maintained against the parties arrested, and all of them, with one exception, were released after various periods of unjustifiable incarceration.

At the conclusion of his indictment against the New York City authorities and their police, Swinton proposed that "the Police Board, which perpetrated these cruel, flagrant, and horrible outrages against the unemployed and suffering workmen of New York," be abolished and a new board created, to be elected by popular vote.

In July 1877, during strikes on the railroads and in other industries, Swinton addressed another huge demonstration in Tompkins Square. A contemporary account says that it was a perilous time for oratory; his friends firmly believed that he was endangering his life and urged him to keep away from the meeting. Nonetheless, he appeared, and he began his address with these words: "With eight thousand rifles and twelve hundred clubs drawn upon me...." This time there was no interference by the police.

In the fall of that year Swinton ran for mayor of New York on the Industrial Political Party ticket. Thirteen years later, as the candidate of the Progressive Labor Party for state senator, he would once again wage a vigorous campaign.

Swinton was not alone in his denunciation of contemporary outrages. Two other former printers, William Dean Howells and Mark Twain, expressed themselves emphatically on the issues of the day. Howells, who in 1871 assumed the editorship of the *Atlantic Monthly*, then the most influential literary journal in America, published articles on the causes of the depression of 1873–1879, and on civil-service reform, immigration, and women's rights.

"An article on 'Children's Labor,'" Robert L. Hough writes in *The Quiet Rebel*, "is particularly arresting in its description of the evils of child labor and the frank admission that such work is necessary to sustain some families."[6] In December 1880, just before he left the *Atlantic*, Howells accepted for publication "The Story of a Great Monopoly," Henry Demarest Lloyd's exposé of the ruthless practices of the Standard Oil Company, a forerunner of "muckraking" articles by Ida M. Tarbell, Ray Stannard Baker, Lincoln Steffens, and John Reed.

Howells wrote Mark Twain on April 5, 1888, commenting on articles Twain had written about the labor movement:

> My dear Clemens:
>
> I have read your two essays with thrills almost amounting to yells of satisfaction. It is about the best thing yet said on the subject; but it is strange that you can't get a single newspaper to face the facts of the situation. Here the fools are now all shouting because the Knights of Labor have revenged themselves on the Engineers, and the

> C. B. and Q. strike is a failure.* No one notices how labor has educated itself; no one perceives that *next* time there won't be any revenge or any failure! If ever a public was betrayed by its press, it's ours. No man could safely make himself heard in behalf of the strikers any more than for the Anarchists.[7]

The "Anarchists" were the Chicago labor organizers who, because they fought for the eight-hour day, were convicted of murder in 1886. Howells, America's most eminent literary figure, "was deeply stirred by the case," writes Alan Calmer. "Although he feared his reputation and livelihood would be jeopardized, he interceded in their behalf."†[8]

The critical sentiments expressed by Howells, Twain, and Swinton found an echo from time to time even in academic circles. Recalling that period in his autobiography, Professor Richard T. Ely of the University of Wisconsin, one of the first labor economists in the United States, and, in his early years, an academic maverick, observes:

> In the last quarter of the nineteenth century the American people witnessed a crisis in the labor movement. It was marked by a deep stirring of the masses—not a local stirring, not merely a national stirring, but an international, worldwide stirring of the masses. The manner of producing

*When the Knights of Labor struck the Philadelphia and Reading Railroad in December 1887, members of the Brotherhood of Locomotive Engineers filled the strikers' jobs; when the Brotherhood struck the Chicago, Burlington, and Quincy, in March 1888, the newspapers charged that Knights of Labor members had acted as strikebreakers.

†See "William Dean Howells and the Haymarket Era," in this volume.

> material goods was examined critically and pronounced faulty. The distribution of these goods among the various members of the social organism was also critically examined and pronounced iniquitous. Proposals were made for new modes of production and distribution of economic goods. The masses desired changes not merely in surface phenomena, but in the very foundation of the social order.[9]

A major event in Swinton's life, and one to which he would make frequent reference, was his meeting with Karl Marx in August 1880, at the seaside resort of Ramsgate, in England. The interview appeared on page 1 of the *New York Sun* on September 6, 1880, and was later published in *John Swinton's Travels: Current Views and Notes of Forty Days in France and England.* His impressions of the founder of scientific Socialism—"one of the most remarkable men of the day"—provide a fascinating glimpse of Marx and his family.* Swinton described Marx in these words:

"A man without desire for fame, caring nothing for the fanfaronade of life or the pretense of power; without haste and without rest, a man of strong, broad, elevated mind, full of far-reaching projects, logical methods, and practical aims, he has stood and yet stands behind more of the earthquakes which have convulsed nations and destroyed thrones, and do now menace and appall crowned heads and established frauds, than any other man in Europe, not excepting Joseph Mazzini himself."

That Swinton could conceive the impact of Marx's philosophy on the world, and view the man and his work with

*For the full text of this interview, see Appendix A.

exaltation, is a tribute not only to his intellectual capacities, but to his scale of values.

Swinton's friend and biographer, Robert Waters, reports a conversation with Swinton about Marx, and quotes him as saying: "I met him in London, and I consider him one of the noblest and most logical thinkers I ever knew. When I became an editor and saw how fortunes were made by a turn of the hand, by secret combinations of capitalists, and how this tended to impoverish the community, I began to see that the whole thing was wrong and that the entire system ought to be changed."

Swinton went on to say, according to Waters: "I made the acquaintance of Wendell Phillips and, found that he, too, had come to similar conclusions. He believed that the capitalist system was steadily undermining the world... and bringing his countrymen into a condition quite as wretched as that of the Negro slaves; and he vehemently condemned it."[10]

Not long after his meeting with Marx in England, Swinton received from him a copy of the French edition of *Capital* and a letter, dated November 4, 1880, thanking him "for your friendly article in the *Sun*," a reference to the interview. The letter was written in English. After reporting that "political interest centers here at present on the Irish 'Land Question,'" Marx told Swinton of the persecutions that had occurred as a result of the anti-Socialist law of the German chancellor, Otto von Bismarck.

"Liebknecht has to enter prison for six months," Marx wrote. "The anti-Socialist law having failed to overthrow or even weaken the German Social Democratic organization, Bismarck clings more desperately to his panacea, and fancies that it *must* work, if only applied on a larger scale. The anti-Socialist law, though it could not break and never will break our organization, does impose pecuniary sacrifices almost impossible to bear. To support the families ruined by the police, to keep alive the few papers left to us, to keep up the necessary communications by secret messengers, to fight the battle on the whole line—all this requires money. We are nearly exhausted and forced to appeal to our friends and sympathizers in other countries."

Assuring Swinton that "we here in London, Paris, etc., will do our best," Marx called upon the American for assistance. "I believe that a man of your influence," he wrote, "might organize a subscription in the United States." He added: "Even if the monetary result were not important, denunciations of Bismarck's new *coup d'état* in public meetings held by you, reported in the American press, reproduced on the other side of the Atlantic, would sorely hit the Pomeranian hobereau [country squire] and be welcomed by all the Socialists of Europe." Marx suggested that for further details Swinton get in touch with Friedrich Sorge, general secretary of the International Workingmen's Association, who lived at that time in Hoboken, New Jersey.

In the same letter—recalling the time they had met in England—Marx wrote: "My youngest daughter [Eleanor]—who was not at Ramsgate—tells me she has cut my portrait from the copy of *Capital* I sent you, on the pretext that it was a mere caricature. Well, I shall make up for it by a photogram to be taken on the first fine day. Mrs. Marx and the whole family send you their best wishes."

A second letter, dated June 2, 1881, and also written in English, was delivered by a refugee from tsarist persecution in Russia, Leo Hartmann, whom Marx commended to Swinton's attention.

"I send you through him a photograph of mine; it is rather

bad, but the only one left to me," Marx wrote. Commenting on Henry George's *Progress and Poverty*, he observed: "I consider it as a last attempt to save the capitalistic regime. Of course, this is not the meaning of the author, but the older disciples of Ricardo—the radical ones—fancied already that by the public appropriation of the rent of land everything would be righted. I have referred to this doctrine in the *Misère de la Philosophie* [*The Poverty of Philosophy*, 1847], against Proudhon.

"Mrs. Marx sends you her best compliments. Unfortunately, her illness assumes more and more a fatal character."

In a letter to Sorge dated November 5, 1880, Marx wrote: "As a result of Bismarck's new state-of-siege decrees and the persecution of our party organs, it is absolutely necessary to raise money for the party. I have therefore written to John Swinton (for a well-meaning bourgeois is best suited to this purpose), and told him to apply to you for detailed information regarding German conditions."[11]

Swinton's role in organizing the movement against Bismarck's anti-Socialist law in the United States is illuminated in an article by Philip S. Foner in the *International Review of Social History*. Referring to Marx's letter asking for financial assistance, Foner writes:

> There is no evidence either that Swinton ever replied to Marx, or that he and Sorge ever contacted each other. But Sorge did inform Marx that he had learned that Swinton had revealed that he had received a letter from Marx, but had said he could do nothing in the matter other than to contribute about $100 personally to the cause. Actually, while Marx did not mention it, Bismarck's anti-Socialist policy had, from its very

> inception, aroused considerable indignation in this country from Socialists, non-Socialist workers, and liberal intellectuals. It took the form of protest meetings and the raising of funds for the relief of the victims of Bismarckism. Swinton himself was a leading figure in these protests.

As an example of this activity, Foner cites a meeting held in Chickering Hall, in New York City, where Swinton not only presided but delivered the main address. After the management had agreed to rent its facilities, Swinton observed that Socialists "had been routed out of First Avenue, clubbed out of Tompkins Square, and subjected to the most infamous outrages in the Democratic regions of the East Side, and now they propose to establish their headquarters in the avenue of the aristocracy [Fifth Avenue]."[12]

Shortly after Marx's death a memorial meeting was held at Cooper Union, in New York, on March 20, 1883. Many nationalities were represented, both on the platform and in the audience, and speeches were made in various languages. Foner describes it as "the outstanding memorial event held anywhere in the world in the weeks immediately following Marx's death." Because of Swinton's celebrated interview with Marx, and the correspondence that followed, it was most appropriate that he be one of the speakers.

The *New York Sun* of March 21 headlined the event: "Tributes to Karl Marx—A Great International Memorial Meeting of Workingmen—Thousands Turned Away from the Doors of Cooper Union—Addresses in English, German, Russian, Bohemian, and French." The *Sun* reported, "If the great hall of Cooper Union had been twice as large as it is, it could not have held the vast throng of workingmen who gathered last evening to do honor to the memory of Dr. Karl Marx."

Introduced to loud applause, Swinton opened his speech with these words: "It is to make requiem for Karl Marx, who has just left the world, that we are here tonight." Quoting from his interview with Marx, he declared that the author of *Capital* was "an observer of American action, and his remarks upon some of the formative and substantive forces of American life were full of suggestiveness." Swinton then summed up his estimate of Marx:

> *Firstly:* Karl Marx was a man of lofty mind, true and free, equipped with all the knowledge of the times.
>
> *Secondly:* It was by his moral nature, his generous and radiant qualities, his faith in right and love of man, that his mind was controlled.
>
> *Thirdly:* Karl Marx did extraordinary work in the world, and when the history of the last forty years is revealed, and the movements of which he was promoter, and which are now in progress throughout Europe, are brought to their consummation, the depth and scope of his work will be known.
>
> *Fourthly:* Karl Marx proclaimed fruitful ideas to mankind—the comprehensive ideas of unity and self-help incarnated in the International Association that have become watchwords of the world's workers; the creative ideas upon political economy, social forces, industrial cooperation, and public law that are found in his *Capital*, and the other great underlying ideas of the Revolution whose star will soon appear over Europe.

> *Fifthly:* Karl Marx gave up his whole life for the disinherited, neglecting the personal ends he might have subserved and the prizes he might have won, rendering himself liable to the hostility of power, by which he was made an outlaw.
>
> *Finally:* In giving all to mankind, Karl Marx gave that which was more than aught else when he gave himself.[13]

Convinced that the true story of labor did not reach working people, Swinton launched his own weekly, *John Swinton's Paper*, on October 14, 1883. A statement of principles set forth its objectives:

1. Boldly upholding the rights of Man in the American Way.
2. Battling against the Accumulated Wrongs of Society and Industry.
3. Striving for the Organization and Interests of Working men and giving the news of the Trades and Unions.
4. Uniting the Political Forces, searching for a common platform, and giving the news of all the Young Bodies in the field.
5. Warning the American people against the treasonable and crushing schemes of Millionaires, Monopolists, and Plutocrats, and against the coming Billionaire whose shadow is now looming up.
6. Looking toward better times of fair play and Public Welfare.

Some typical headlines in *John Swinton's Paper* were: "Millionaire Dodgers Must Be Forced to Pay Their Share of Taxes—Put an End to the Swindling and Perjury of the Giants Who Devour Us"; "The Working Women—100,000 of Them Struggling Through Life in This City."

Coverage was not limited to the local scene. A headline in the issue of February 2, 1885, read: "England and Ireland: Scope of the New Struggle Against Landlordism."

Editorials were pithy. News dispatches were brisk. There were also advertisements, but not from big business. Most were from booksellers and other small tradesmen.

Regular departments included "Trade Unions in the City" and "Meetings of the Unions." One issue carried a story by a staff writer titled "Two Nights in Poe's Room in Fordham," a genial essay on William Dean Howells, and a list of recommended books and magazines. Another issue contained a number of poems and a sketch by Émile Zola.

The August 31, 1884, issue of the paper announced: "We have made arrangements with Mrs. Eleanor Marx-Aveling, the daughter of the late Karl Marx, for a series of letters from London. We shall next week give the first of them, which has just come to hand, and which contains some interesting news about the books left by her distinguished father, now under preparation for the publisher in London."

And, indeed, in the next week's issue of *John Swinton's Paper* (September 7, 1884) a full column of correspondence from Eleanor Marx was featured. It was headlined: "Karl Marx's Daughter—The Second Volume of Her Father's Great Work Left Complete—His Life-Long Toil." She wrote:

> Not only Socialists, but all students of political economy, are looking forward with interest and impatience to the publication in English of Karl Marx's *Das Kapital.* A translation is now in progress of which, at some future date, I shall be

> glad to give full details. At present I can only say that the work is in able and loving hands and that it probably will appear in two volumes by next Spring.
>
> The two greatest thinkers of the age, Charles Darwin and Karl Marx, who had so many qualities in common, were both special examples of the capacity of genius for taking infinite pains. Both of these men will be remembered for their germinal discoveries that revolutionized natural science and the science of political economy—the one leading the quiet life of the scientific discoverer, the other the stormy life of the revolutionist, but both always true to themselves and to their work.
>
> I like to remember—I do not think it has ever before been noted—that *The Origin of Species* and the *Kritik der Politischen Ökonomie* (which contains the germs of the theories more fully developed in *Das Kapital*) were both given to the world in 1859.

Five weeks later (October 12, 1884) Swinton published another dispatch from Eleanor Marx. Under the headline "Marx's Daughter—Half a Million Men Idle in England, as Many Half-Idle," she reported, "Besides some half million laborers entirely out of work (in England alone), at least 500,000 men are on half time, and those who know what the starvation wages of 'full time' mean will readily understand that we are face to face with an immense crisis."

The news items and editorials in *John Swinton's Paper* denounced low wages, the high cost of living, discrimination in women workers' rates of pay, judges who granted injunctions against labor-organizing and strikes, and congressmen who opposed a bill to establish a bureau of labor standards. A special Washington correspondent contributed an article headlined: "Bulwark of Capital—The Millionaires Who Rule the Senate—Living Sketches of Dried Specimens."

Dispatches from industrial centers described "the bitter lot of labor" in the mills and mines: "If Villard cannot afford the wages paid to his hands on the Northern Pacific Railroad, how can he afford to go on with the building of his million-dollar palace in this city? If Cyrus W. Field cannot afford to pay his janitors more than $4 a week, how can he afford to feast all the British aristocracy?"

John Swinton's Paper gave considerable attention to the condition of women and children, not only in editorials and articles but also in letters from workers in various industries. In the issue of March 8, 1885, one headline read "Little Mill Slaves—New Child Labor Bill in the New York State Legislature—Steps Proposed to Modify the Satanic System Under Which Thousands of Children Are Murdered Every Year." Swinton's correspondent in Albany reported that the measure would apply to places "where machinery propelled by steam, water, or other mechanical power is used." The first section of the proposed bill stipulated that no one under twenty-one "shall be employed for more than ten hours a day."

In "A Woman and Her Sisters," a garment worker told about "a certain suit company on 14th Street," in New York City. "Previous to June," she said, "the girls had received from 90 cents to $1.50 for an entire suit, and 65 cents for ladies' wrappers. The workers are often asked, 'Why don't you refuse such prices?' Because they [the employers] would only say to us: 'Go! if you are not satisfied.'"

Another woman gave this account: "The shop in which I work employs sometimes as many as a hundred girls, but as 'business is dull,' just now we have no more than thirty at work. Our employer and her sister treat us like dogs: 'What do you mean by such work as this, Miss ——?' We have all countries represented: about half the girls are Germans, about a quarter Irish or Irish-American, and the rest are 'Ninth Warders,' that means Americans."

In his November 1, 1885, editorial Swinton praised the New York Central Labor Union for bringing before the public "some of the more grievous wrongs of the women—mostly young women.... It is noble work that has been undertaken by the Central Labor Union of this city for protecting the working women of the various trades against the countless wrongs to which they are subject under our cruel industrial system."

A page-one dispatch from Pittsburgh on September 14, 1884, headlined "Brave Women of the Mines," described a meeting of miners' wives and their resolve to "stand by their husbands," who had been jailed for strike activities. In February 1885, according to Foner's *History of the Labor Movement in the United States*, a dinner was held to honor three women carpet-weavers from Yonkers who had been arrested for picketing while twenty-five hundred women were striking to protest the firing of Knights of Labor members. The entire labor movement of New York City joined in this tribute, and John Swinton "had been designated to present them with medals in honor of their militancy and courage."[14]

A direct question on women's rights was put to Swinton by a reader from Columbus, Ohio, in the issue of November 4, 1886. Addressing her letter "To the Editor," she wrote: "In my wishes of good speed for your success in establishing 'the rights of man in the American way' [the first point in the statement of principles of *John Swinton's Paper*], I with others wish to know if women are to be placed upon your platform with equal rights and privileges, and to have fair play in the better time that your faithful labor must bring."

Swinton replied: "Most assuredly. When we speak of the rights of man, those of woman are implied every time, truly and fully—her right to life, liberty, and the pursuit of happiness.... In the great productive industries into which millions of women are now being driven, the Knights of Labor are steadily striving to secure the enforcement of the following great principle of their platform: 'To secure for both sexes equal pay for equal work.' This is not a mere empty demand, such as might be put out by double-faced politicians; it is meant to take practical shape. Women are not only invited to membership in the Knights of Labor, but they are eligible to all offices of the Order. Fair play for woman every time!"

Swinton's sensitivity to the problems of the black workers of his time is revealed in an editorial of November 28, 1886, "A Mistake of Colored Men." A correspondent in Missouri, he wrote, had told of miners who were "supplanted by colored men," as strikebreakers. Commenting on this incident, Swinton said that impoverished black men "were transferred from the South by the corporation," and he compared this practice to the contract system of imported labor.

Swinton declared: "It is hard to find fault with the poor colored men for the part they have taken in these inroads; but for the capitalists who have brought them to the North, there should be nothing short of positive public condemnation. In the country districts of the South, the Negro laborers are held in a condition akin to slavery. They are paid so little wages, receive so little cash after their fifty or seventy-five cents a day suffers from the 'pluck me' system [company stores], that they are easily lured to the North at wages disgustingly inadequate for white workingmen. The imposition on the Negroes is systematically carried out." Swinton concluded his editorial by denouncing the system of convict labor in the South, where black men were sentenced to "ten and twenty years for petty crimes" for which whites would not even have been charged.

Unfortunately, Swinton did not display the same keen sympathies on the issue of Chinese immigration. His views on the subject were first presented in the *New York Tribune* of June 30, 1870. What had precipitated this article was the importation that year of Chinese to work in a shoe factory in North Adams, Massachusetts. This was seen as a threat to unionism and to the movement for the eight-hour day. According to Dr. Marc Ross, however, Swinton's opposition to the importation of Chinese laborers "seems to have been impelled more by a desire to protect American civilization from the intrusion of an alien and unassimilable population than by the implications of their importation for the conditions of labor of American workers."[15]

"There is reason to dread the infusion and transfusion of the Chinese, Mongolian, or Yellow race with the white American race," Swinton had written in *The New Issue: The Chinese-American Question*, a pamphlet published in 1870. And in his own paper he had proclaimed, "The Chinese must go; no more mongolization in our country." Although Swinton argued that an influx of Chinese laborers would depress the wages of native workingmen, his language was undeniably racist; in this he failed to rise above his times and above those who had denigrated the common humanity first of the enslaved blacks and then of the free "people of color."

On August 7, 1887, there appeared this announcement in Swinton's publication: "For almost four years, at a heavy expense to myself, for every week of each year, I have edited and published *John Swinton's Paper.* My means are no longer sufficient to bear any further strain. . . . I have sunk tens of thousands of dollars—all of it out of my own pocket. In the final number, a fortnight hence, I shall give a review of the past and present for the information of all friends—to whom I shall then bid Farewell!"

Unexpired subscriptions would be credited to another paper, Swinton promised, and any sums due to advertisers who had paid in advance would be refunded at once.

The final issue of *John Swinton's Paper*, on August 21, 1887, carried this valedictory:

> FAREWELL!
> To my many faithful friends and sturdy fellow workers all over this broad land, who have stood by me in this paper, aiding the work it was founded to promote, or cherishing the principles which it has steadily proclaimed—I now bid FAREWELL.
>
> John Swinton

Two years earlier Swinton had indicated some of the hardships he had faced as a labor editor when he declared: "There are American wage-workers, descended from Revolutionary sires, who dare not take this paper for fear of the employers. Several men think it is safer to get the paper in roundabout ways, or at post-offices distant from their homes. To be caught with it in some of the slave mills of New England would cost a man as much as his wages are worth."

One day someone who asked Swinton if he made money on his paper got this reply: "Did you ever hear of Washington, or Luther, or Garrison, making money by their work? No, sir; only mercenaries live to make money."[16] Nevertheless, he had to have cash to operate. After the paper had been in existence for sixteen months, he made a special appeal to his readers, and evidently they responded. The paper was published for two more years. Swinton ultimately put forty thousand dollars of his savings into it.

Professor Selig Perlman, labor historian at the University of Wisconsin, called *John Swinton's Paper* "the best labor paper printed in the country's history."[17] Eugene V. Debs wrote: "It was a paper of remarkable ability and force, and by far the best radical paper then in existence, but it had to succumb at last. It was a menace to Wall Street and the monied interests, and they finally succeeded in forcing it to the wall."[18]

On the basis of his experience as a journalist, Swinton had harsh words for the newspaper business. "Journalism, once a profession, and then a trade, is now a crime," he is said to have remarked on one occasion. Upton Sinclair, in *The Cry for Justice: An Anthology of Social Protest* (1915), wrote that Swinton, "one of America's oldest and most beloved journalists," startled his fellow editors, at a banquet in his honor, by this response to a toast to the "independent press":

> There is no such thing in America as an independent press, unless it is in the country towns. You know it and I know it. There is not one of you who dares write his honest opinions, and if you did, you know beforehand that it would never appear in print.

> I am paid $150 a week for keeping my honest opinions out of the paper I am connected with. Others of you are paid similar salaries for similar things, and any of you who would be so foolish as to write his honest opinions would be out on the streets looking for another job.
>
> The business of the New York journalist is to destroy the truth, to lie outright, to pervert, to vilify, to fawn at the feet of Mammon, and to sell his race and his country for his daily bread.
>
> You know this and I know it, and what folly is this to be toasting an "independent press."
>
> We are the tools and vassals of rich men behind the scenes. We are the jumping-jacks; they pull the strings and we dance. Our talents, our possibilities, and our lives are all the property of other men. We are intellectual prostitutes.

Sinclair said, "I speak not in my own voice but in that of an old-time journalist, venerated in his day, John Swinton."[19] But Dr. Marc Ross notes that in the May 1960 *Bulletin of the American Society of Newspaper Editors*, Chester M. Lewis, director of the *New York Times* archives, wrote that he could not locate the original source of the remarks. Sinclair told Lewis: "That Swinton quote haunted me for forty years. It was a sort of classic in the Socialist movement. I had seen it often and took it for granted."[20] He included it in every edition of *The Cry for Justice* and in his exposé of the press, *The Brass Check* (1920). He may have read it first in the *Chicago Labor Enquirer* of May 12, 1888, where Swinton is identified in the same words that Sinclair later used; the byline is "John Swinton" rather than a reporter's name.

At the 1892 convention of the American Federation of Labor in Philadelphia, Swinton spoke of "the battalions that fought this year at Homestead, Buffalo, and Coeur d'Alene." He urged the delegates to find some way of "unifying the industrial and productive elements of the country for defense against dangers that are all too obvious," asking urgently, "Can we not agree upon some one thing while differing upon other things?" He suggested, "It is time for the struggling working people of the Eastern states to link arms with the advancing farmers of the resurgent West."

At workers' gatherings Swinton was generally among the speakers on the platform, but one night in the fall of 1894 he was in the audience at Cooper Union when the speaker was Eugene V. Debs, awaiting trial for defying an injunction against the Pullman strike (he was convicted in 1895 and jailed for six months). Thirty-four years earlier, Swinton had listened to another gaunt man from the Midwest speaking from the same platform, and now he was moved to make this observation: "Debs in Cooper Union reminded me of Lincoln there. As Lincoln of Illinois became an efficient agent for freedom, so, perchance, might Debs of Indiana become in the impending conflict for the liberation of labor. Let us never forget Lincoln's great words, 'Liberty before property, the man before the dollar.'"[21]

Swinton and Debs became friends, and the respect and affection between them were profound. Debs later wrote: "Swinton, who might have had unlimited wealth and power and 'fame,' died in poverty and almost in obscurity, because he was truly great and uncompromisingly honest, scorning to barter his principles and convictions for a gilded cage and a life-lease of pampered self-indulgence to soften his brain, eat out his heart, and petrify his soul."

Swinton's speeches, said Debs, "were scholarly in thought, classical in composition, and contained some of the most thrilling passages to be found in American oratory." Swinton, like his friend Wendell Phillips, "understood the labor question in its deeper significance and wider aspects; he had a clear grasp of its fundamental principles and its international scope and character, and he knew that the labor movement was revolutionary and that its mission of emancipating the working class from wage slavery could be accomplished only by destroying the system and reorganizing society upon a new economic foundation."

Describing the many warm letters he had received from Swinton, Debs said that they were "filled with kindness, with loyalty and greetings of good cheer." During the Pullman strike, when Debs was facing prison, Swinton wrote, "You are waging a Napoleonic battle amidst the admiration of millions. Be strong, Brother Debs!" In June 1897, Debs told him, "The railroad managers have sworn that the American Railway Union should not be organized and their detectives are dogging my footsteps by day and night." Swinton replied: "The strength of your faith, the liveliness of your hopes, the persistency of your valor, the breadth of your thought, and the energy of your genius fill me with admiration. These things belong to that kind of Americanism which is ever regenerative."

Whenever he was in New York, Debs saw Swinton: "The little visits we had together were occasions of special enjoyment and delight to me. He had the reputation of being somewhat brusque in manner, but I never found him so. On the contrary, he was always genial as sunshine to me. At his home he was the very soul of hospitality. He lived modestly with his wife, whom he addressed as 'Angel' and in whom he had a most sympathetic and helpful companion in all his arduous labors and disappointing experiences."

Like many radicals of the time, Debs was enormously impressed by Swinton's interview with Marx: "He visited Karl Marx, and it may readily be imagined that these two great revolutionary souls found genial companionship in each other. . . . Both Marx and Swinton are gone, but their work remains and the heroic, unselfish examples they set will be a perpetual inspiration to the world." Swinton and Marx saw struggle ahead, Debs said, writing during World War I: "The years which have followed have amply vindicated their prescience. Struggle there has been over all the face of the earth, increasing steadily in violence and intensity until today the whole of humanity seems seized with a madness for bloodshed and destruction that threatens an upheaval wide as the world and unparalleled in the world's history."[22]

A Debs-like spirit animates Swinton's *Striking for Life: Labor's Side of the Labor Question* (1894).* In this stirring volume, he wrote: "It is most certainly an unsatisfactory and unpromising outlook under the existing state of things. But it must be possible for the American people to make up their mind that these mighty agencies—new forces and new appliances of inventive skill—shall be used for public advantage rather than for private enrichment; for the welfare of the community, rather than for its impoverishment."[23]

*In addition to thirty-three chapters by Swinton, the book contains a number of his speeches; articles by Debs, by Samuel Gompers of the American Federation of Labor, and by John W. Hayes of the Knights of Labor; and many photographs and documents relating to the labor movement. It was reprinted in 1895 with the new title *A Momentous Question: The Respective Attitudes of Labor and Capital.*

An equally good friend was Walt Whitman. They had known each other since 1855, and the bond between them became even closer when together they visited the Civil War wounded. Some years later, Swinton wrote:

> I saw him time and again, in the Washington hospitals, or wending his way there with basket or haversack on his arm; and the strength of beneficence suffusing his face. His devotion surpassed the devotion of woman. It would take a volume to tell of his kindness, tenderness, and thoughtfulness.
>
> Never shall I forget one night when I accompanied him on his rounds through a hospital, filled with those wounded young Americans whose heroism he has sung in deathless numbers. There were three rows of cots, and each cot bore its man. When he appeared, in passing along there was a smile of affection and welcome on every face, however wan, and his presence seemed to light up the place as it might be lit by the presence of the Son of Love. From cot to cot they called him often in tremulous tones or in whispers; they embraced him, they touched his hand, they gazed at him. To one he gave a few words of cheer, for another he wrote a letter home, to others he gave an orange, a few comfits, a cigar, a pipe and tobacco, a sheet of paper or a postage stamp, all of which and many other things were in his capacious haversack.
>
> From another he would receive a dying message for mother, wife, or sweetheart; for another he would promise to go an errand; to another,

> some special friend, very low, he would give a manly farewell kiss. He did the things for them which no nurse or doctor could do, and he seemed to leave a benediction at every cot as he passed along. The lights had gleamed for hours in the hospital that night before he left it, and as he took his way towards the door, you could hear the voice of many a stricken hero calling, "Walt, Walt, Walt, come again! come again!"
>
> His basket and stores, filled with all sorts of odds and ends for the men, had been emptied. He had really little to give, but it seemed to me as though he gave more than other men.[24]

On September 25, 1868, Swinton told Whitman of his enthusiasm for *Leaves of Grass*: "My dear and great Walt. I want to see you that I may get another copy of the *Leaves* and subscribe an X for expense of publication. I am profoundly impressed with the great humanity or genius that expresses itself through you.... I could convey no idea to you how it affects my soul. It is more to me than all other books and poetry."[25] (The first and second editions of *Leaves of Grass* [1855, 1856] had been published by Orsena Swinton's father, the phrenologist Orson Squire Fowler.)

A passionate admirer of Whitman's writings, Swinton helped to bring his books to the attention of the public. On October 1, 1868, for example, the following item appeared in the "Minor Topics" column that Swinton conducted in the *New York Times*: "With the bright, crispy Autumn weather Walt Whitman again makes his appearance on the sidewalks of Broadway. His large, massive personality—his grave and prophetic yet free and manly appearance—his insouciance of manner and movement—his easy and negligent yet clean and wholesome dress—make up a figure of an individuality that attracts the attention of every passer-by."

The article then informed readers of the growth of Whitman's reputation abroad: "Rossetti has classed him with Homer and one or two other great poetic geniuses of the world." Moreover, the famous German poet Ferdinand Freiligrath, a friend of Marx's, was planning to translate *Leaves of Grass.* The item concluded with the announcement of the forthcoming publication of "a small work in prose," *Democratic Vistas.*[26]

Swinton did not confine himself to publicizing Whitman's writings; he helped promote them in a most practical way, sending Whitman printed forms for potential purchasers of books, editions of which the poet sold by subscription for some twenty years. A note "to various friends" said: "In a letter from my friend John Swinton, he speaks of your kind desire to subscribe for some copies.... I send you enclosed slips. Of course I should be happy to furnish you with any copies. I am still jogging along here in the two-thirds ill, one-third well condition of these late years."[27]

It was through Swinton that *Leaves* of Grass was first brought to the attention of Russian readers. In August 1882, a translation of a lecture on American literature that he had delivered before a German society in New York City and before the Philosophical Society of Williamsburg, in Brooklyn, appeared in the *Zagranichny Vyestnik* (*Foreign Herald*).[28] Swinton wrote Whitman, "Now I have the magazine and you have a very heavy puff in the organ which is studied by all the powerful and intellectual classes of Russia."

Whitman's close friend Horace Traubel, in his book *With Walt Whitman in Camden*, wrote that Whitman asked him to read the letter aloud, and when he had finished the poet said: "That has a real sound. It seems to take me way off into a strange country, and set me down there.... I'm as much for all countries as for one and I suppose I am so that I should not feel like an alien even over in that great Tartar Empire."

Swinton often expressed the view that labor's progress was slow. Traubel recalled Whitman saying: "Swinton sometimes seems to get in the dumps awful.... He is down in the mouth about the tardiness of the people to respond to the appeal of the economic radicals." And Traubel commented, "The people will come along in their own time—yes, and take their time."[29]

One day in April 1888, while chatting with Whitman, Traubel mentioned Swinton. Whitman replied, "John, you know, is stormy, tempestuous—raises a hell of a row over things—yet underneath all is nothing that is not noble, sweet, sane." These remarks were prompted by the turning-up of a letter that Swinton had written him in 1874, described by Whitman as "almost like a love letter" but not unusual in the fervid rhetoric of the day:

> *My beloved Walt*: I have read the sublime poem of the Universal once and again, and yet again—seeing it in the *Graphic*, *Post*, *Mail*, *World*, and many other papers. It is sublime. It raised my mind to its own sublimity. It seems to me the sublimest of all your poems. I cannot help reading it every once of a while. I return to it as a fountain of joy.
>
> My beloved Walt: You know how I have worshipped you, without change or cessation, for twenty years. While my soul exists, that worship must be ever new.

It was perhaps the very day of the publication of the first edition of the *Leaves of Grass* that I saw a copy of it at a newspaper stand in Fulton Street, Brooklyn. I got it, looked into it with wonder, and felt that here was something that touched the depths of my humanity. Since then you have grown before me, grown around me, and grown into me.

I expected certainly to go down to Camden last fall to see you. But something prevented. And, in time I saw in the papers that you had recovered. The New Year took me into a new field of action among the miserables. Oh, what scenes of human horror were to be found in this city last winter. I cannot tell you how much I was engaged, or all I did for three months. I must wait till I see you to tell you about these things. I have been going toward social radicalism of late years and appeared here at the Academy of Music as president and orator of the Rochefort meeting.* Now I would like to see you, in order to temper my heart, and expand my narrowness.

How absurd it is to suppose that there is any ailment in the brain of a man who can generate the poem of the Universal. I would parody Lincoln and say that such kind of ailment ought to spread.†

*Victor-Henri, marquis de Rochefort, a journalist, escaped from the penal colony where he had been sent for supporting the Paris Commune.

†To complaints about General Ulysses S. Grant's drinking, Lincoln is said to have replied that, in view of Grant's military genius, he wished the same ailment would spread to all of his generals.

> My beloved Walt. Tell me if you would like me to come to see you, and perhaps I can do so within a few weeks.

Traubel said: "I quoted W. that phrase from Swinton's letter, 'I have been going toward social radicalism of late years.' 'Yes,' said W., 'I remember it. Are we not all going that way or already gone?' "[30]

Despite his intense admiration for Marx, Swinton was not a scientific Socialist. His outlook was close to that of the utopian Socialists of the time. His ardor was all for labor's cause; his talents as a journalist were dedicated to working people. His eyes had been opened to many of the evils of American capitalist society; his passionate reaction to these evils made him a forerunner of the "muckrakers" of the next generation. In his book *Striking for Life*, he declared:

> It is not possible for the masses of our country to prosper so long as the main part of its resources are seized by the insatiable rich, or so long as the currents of wealth continue to flow in the direction which they have taken within recent times....
>
> Something more than small reforms are now necessary. Something else than legislation like that in which Congress habitually indulges is imperative. Something other than the bogus philanthropies of the plundering classes is essential to the public salvation....
>
> All this is within the range of good and orderly business. It can be done without the violation of any law of life or nature. It can be done peacefully, safely, and without long delay or extrava-

> gance. It can be done without going beyond the powers justly held by the community, and without violating any fundamental principle of our Federal Constitution—a document, by the way, which has been wrested from its true uses in order to subserve the interests of the public enemy.
>
> The primal resources and forces of nature, the fundamental agencies of production and transportation, the apparatus of finance and exchange, the corporate franchises granted by the State—all ought to be the possession of the community in mass, not the means of private aggrandizement.
>
> Such possession would not interfere with the free and full play of any of the worthy powers of man. It would promote the development of all that is valuable in the country. It would establish the general welfare upon a sure and strong foundation.
>
> Toward something of this kind the American people must look, or else they may as well look for a descent from bad to worse.[31]

When his life, work, and development are viewed in their totality, it becomes clear that John Swinton merits greater recognition than has so far been accorded him. He was an outstanding American who not only exposed and fought the venality of the prevailing social system but saw the necessity of, and hoped for, a more humanistic social order.

Appendix A

John Swinton's Interview with Karl Marx (August 1880)*

One of the most remarkable men of the day, who has played an inscrutable but puissant part in the revolutionary politics of the past forty years, is Karl Marx. A man without desire for show or fame, caring nothing for the fanfaronade of life or the pretense of power, without haste and without rest, a man of strong, broad, elevated mind, full of far-reaching projects, logical methods, and practical aims, he has stood and yet stands behind more of the earthquakes which have convulsed nations and destroyed thrones, and do now menace and appall crowned heads and established frauds, than any other man in Europe, not excepting Joseph Mazzini himself.

The student of Berlin, the critic of Hegelianism, the editor of papers, and the old-time correspondent of the *New York Tribune*, he showed his qualities and his spirit; the founder and master spirit of the once-dreaded International, and the author of *Capital*, he has been expelled from half the countries of Europe, proscribed in nearly all of them, and for thirty years past, has found refuge in London. He was at Ramsgate, the great seashore resort of the Londoners,

New York Sun, September 6, 1880; reprinted in *John Swinton's Travels: Current Views and Notes of Forty Days in France and England.*

while I was in London, and there I found him in his cottage, with his family of two generations. The saintly-faced, sweet-voiced, graceful woman of suavity, who welcomed me at the door, was evidently the mistress of the house and the wife of Karl Marx. And is this massive-headed, generous-featured, courtly, kindly man of sixty, with the bushy masses of long, revelling gray hair, Karl Marx?

His dialogue reminded me of that of Socrates—so free, so sweeping, so creative, so incisive, so genuine—with its sardonic touches, its gleams of humor, and its sportive merriment. He spoke of the political forces and popular movements of the various countries of Europe—the vast current of the spirit of Russia, the motions of the German mind, the action of France, the immobility of England. He spoke hopefully of Russia, philosophically of Germany, cheerfully of France, and somberly of England—referring contemptuously to the "atomistic reforms" over which the Liberals of the British Parliament spend their time. Surveying the European world, country after country, indicating the features and the developments and the personages of the surface and under the surface, he showed that things were working toward ends which will assuredly be realized. I was often surprised as he spoke. It was evident that this man, of whom so little is seen or heard, is deep in the times; and that, from the Neva to the Seine, from the Urals to the Pyrenees, his hand is at work preparing the way for the new advent. Nor is his work wasted now any more than it has been in the past, during which so many desirable changes have been brought about, so many heroic struggles have been seen, and the French Republic has been set up on the heights.

As he spoke, the question I had put, "Why are you doing nothing now?" was seen to be a question of the unlearned, and one to which he could not make direct answer. Inquiring why his great work, *Capital*, the seed field of so many crops, had not been put into Russian and French from the original German, he seemed unable to tell, but said that a proposition for an English translation had come to him from New York. He said that that book was but a fragment, a single part of a work in three parts, two of the parts being yet unpublished, the full trilogy being "Land," "Capital," "Credit," the last part, he said, being largely illustrated from the United States, where credit has had such an amazing development. Mr. Marx is an observer of American action, and his remarks upon some of the formative and substantive forces of American life were full of suggestiveness. By the way, in referring to his *Capital*, he said that anyone who might want to read it would find the French translation superior in many ways to the German original. Mr. Marx referred to Henri Rochefort, the Frenchman, and in his talk of some of his dead disciples, the stormy Bakunin, the brilliant Lassalle, and others, I could see how deeply his genius had taken hold of men who, under the circumstances, might have directed the course of history.

The afternoon is waning toward the long twilight of an English summer evening as Mr. Marx discourses, and he proposes a walk through the seaside town and along the shore to the beach, upon which we see many thousand people, largely children disporting themselves. Here we find on the sands his family party—the wife, who had already welcomed me, his two daughters with their children, and his two sons-in-law, one of whom is professor in Kings College, London, and the other, I believe, a man of letters. It was a delightful party—about ten in all—the father of the two young wives, who were happy with their children, and the grandmother of the children, rich in the joysomeness and serenity of her wifely nature. Not less finely than Victor Hugo himself does Karl Marx understand the art of being a grandfather; but more fortunate than Hugo, the married children of Marx live to make jocund his years.

Toward nightfall, he and his sons-in-law part from their families to pass an hour with their American guest. And the talk was of the world, and of man, and of time, and of ideas, as our glasses tinkled over the sea. The railway train waits for no man, and night is at hand. Over the thought of the babblement and rack of the age and the ages, over the talk of the day and the scenes of the evening, arose in my mind one question touching upon the final law of being, for which I would seek answer from this sage. Going down to the depths of language and rising to the height of emphasis, during an interspace of silence, I interrupted the revolutionist and philosopher in these fateful words: "What is?"

And it seemed as though his mind were inverted for a moment while he looked upon the roaring sea in front and the restless multitude upon the beach. "What is?" I had inquired, to which, in deep and solemn tone, he replied: "Struggle!" At first it seemed as though I had heard the echo of despair: but peradventure it was the law of life.

Appendix B

Karl Marx's Comments on the Translating of *Das Kapital* by John Swinton*

There is a rumpus among the disciples of Karl Marx in London about the translating from German into English of his masterpiece, *Capital.* It has just been translated by John Broadhouse, and is now being published piecemeal, in the London magazine the *Day.* But Frederick Engels, one of Mr. Marx's literary executors, has fired a broadside into Broadhouse's translation. He shows that Broadhouse has an imperfect knowledge of German, with a feeble command of English, and that he is wholly unfitted to translate this most untranslatable of German prose writers.

This squabble recalls to my mind the remarks made to me about the translation of *Capital* by Karl Marx himself, when I spent an afternoon with him at the English town of Ramsgate five years ago. Asking him why it had not been put in English as it had been put in French and Russian, from the original German, he replied that a proposition for an English translation had come to him from New York, and then he went on to make other remarks that ought to be of interest to both Broadhouse and Engels. He said that his

**John Swinton's Paper*, November 29, 1885.

German text was often obscure and that it would be found exceedingly difficult to turn it into English. "But look at the translation into French," he said as he presented me with a copy of the Paris edition of *Le Capital*. "That," he continued, "is far clearer, and the style better than the German original. It is from this that the translation into English ought to be made, and I wish you would say so to any one in New York who may try to put the book into English. I really took great pains in revising this French translation [1872–1873], which was made by Joseph Roy; I went over every word of the French manuscript, and much of the language and many of the passages so hard to turn from German into English can be easily translated from the French version. When it is put into English," he repeated, "let the French version be used."

These are the words of Karl Marx himself, which are now for the first time put in print.

A few days ago, in taking up the first chapter of Mr. Broadhouse's translation, my eye fell on a sentence so obscure as to be unintelligible, but in turning to the French version, the meaning of the sentence was plain.

It would seem as though Mr. Marx's literary executors must have heard from his own lips what he said to me in August of 1880.

Charles P. Steinmetz, Scientist and Socialist

Amidst the downward tendency and proneness of things . . . will you not tolerate one or two solitary voices in the land, speaking for thoughts and principles not marketable or perishable?

Ralph Waldo Emerson

Nearly two decades before the Social Security system was established in the United States, a guest lecturer addressed the Economic Club of Boston. "Social insurance—provision for the old, the sick, the unemployed—ought somehow to be achieved," he said. "It should be charged to the overhead expense of industrial processes." The speaker was Charles P. Steinmetz, renowned electrical engineer and Socialist.[1]

Steinmetz was much sought after despite his unconventional political outlook. He was in demand not only by local societies of electrical engineers but by groups interested in his advanced social views, acquired from the study of the writings of Karl Marx, Friedrich Engels, and—in his youthful years—Ferdinand Lassalle.

In 1915, two years prior to his Boston speech, Steinmetz had warned prophetically of the energy crisis we would later face. "Oil and natural gas will long have vanished," he wrote. "Indeed, they may be the first to go." Ultimately, he predicted, only one source of energy will be left, "and that is the energy of sunlight, for this is the greatest of all energies." Steinmetz was concerned about air pollution and the excessive (and wasteful) use of coal and gasoline. He believed that the electric car was the automobile of the future because "it runs cleanly, and quickly, and burns only rechargeable fuel."[2]

Even the briefest contact with Steinmetz, a contemporary observer said, "reveals a singular individuality, and that of a very high order, a man of fine and ready mind and one crammed full of the passion for work, an individuality which combines authority in utterance with a remarkably childlike personal humility."[3]

Charles P. Steinmetz was born on April 9, 1865, in Breslau, Germany (now Wroclaw, Poland). He was christened Karl August Rudolph Steinmetz and confirmed in the Lutheran Church.[4] His father, Karl Heinrich Steinmetz, was employed by the government to prepare railway schedules for the lithographer. His grandfather, German by birth, was an innkeeper in Ostrowo, near the Russian frontier, and had married a Polish woman whose family name was Gawenska. Ostrowo was in a part of Poland that had been acquired by Germany, the other beneficiaries to the dismemberment of the country being Austria and tsarist Russia.[5] Karl's mother, Caroline Neubert Steinmetz, died when he was a year old, and he was reared by his Polish grandmother in Breslau. Born with curvature of the spine, when he grew to manhood he was barely five feet tall.

At the University of Breslau, where fellow students gave him the sobriquet "Proteus" (because he could move from one field of intellectual inquiry to another with the greatest of ease), Steinmetz studied mathematics, physics, chemistry, and astronomy, as well as economics and political science. During his student days he supported himself by tutoring and by writing for German scientific publications. As editor of an illegal Socialist newspaper in Breslau, the *Volksstimme* (*People's Voice*), he attracted the attention of the authorities, who were zealous in their enforcement of the repressive anti-Socialist law promulgated by Bismarck. As a result, he was forced to flee Germany just as he had fulfilled the requirements for his doctoral degree. He had completed work on his dissertation, and it had been accepted. All that remained was the formality of confirming the degree, which he never obtained.

From Breslau, Steinmetz traveled to Zurich, Switzerland, where he enrolled as a student of mechanical engineering at the Federal Institute of Technology—the Eidgenössische Technische Hochschule—in 1888. The following year, when a Socialist named Oscar Asmussen offered to pay his passage across the Atlantic, Steinmetz left Switzerland and journeyed to the United States.

Steinmetz arrived in New York on June 1, 1889, in the steerage section of the French liner *La Champagne*. He was twenty-four years old. Immigration officials were reluctant to admit him into the country. "His distorted body, his poverty and lack of friends here, made him liable to become a 'public charge,'" wrote McAlister Coleman, later a fellow Socialist. However, when his traveling companion, Asmussen, assured the officials at Castle Garden that he would look after his friend, Steinmetz was finally allowed to land.[6]

His writings in technical journals in Germany provided Steinmetz with his first contact in the United States. Ten days after he arrived, he obtained a job with another German émigré, Rudolph Eickemeyer, in Yonkers, New York. Eickemeyer hired him as a draftsman at two dollars a day. Although his employer was an older man, Steinmetz later recalled, their tastes and work were practically the same. Eickemeyer, too, was one of the "dissatisfied," and he had been forced to flee Germany after the Revolution of 1848.

When the recently formed General Electric Company absorbed the Eickemeyer firm three years later, Steinmetz moved with it to Lynn, Massachusetts, where he remained for a year. In 1893 he was transferred to the GE plant in Schenectady. There he was to serve as chief consulting engineer until his death.

A GE executive gave this account of his first impression of Steinmetz:

> I was startled and disappointed by the strange sight of a small, frail body surmounted by a large head, with long hair, hanging to the shoulders, clothed in an old cardigan jacket, cigar in mouth, sitting cross-legged on a laboratory work table. My disappointment was momentary, and completely disappeared the moment he began to talk. I instantly felt the strange power of his piercing but kindly eyes, his enthusiasm, his earnestness. His clear conceptions and marvelous grasp of engineering problems convinced me that we had indeed made a great find. It needed no prophetic insight to realize that here was a man who, if given the opportunity, was destined to render great service to our industry.[7]

In 1892, three years after his arrival in the United States, Steinmetz read two papers before the American Institute of Electrical Engineers which solved a highly specialized technical problem that was impeding the technological development of the electrical industry.* This work brought him worldwide recognition at the age of twenty-seven.

Steinmetz's name is associated with numerous major achievements in electrical engineering. He developed a practical method for making calculations concerning alternating current circuits. (His three volumes on alternating currents have been basic references for years, and another work, *Engineering Mathematics*, was intended for high-school students who planned to enter the electrical-engineering profession.) Steinmetz evolved the theory of "electrical transients," which made it possible for engineers to understand the effects of lightning on high-voltage electrical transmission lines. Once one understands what lightning does to overhead wires, one can take measures to protect the generators and other equipment during a lightning storm. It was his feat of producing artificial lightning in the GE laboratory on March 2, 1922, that prompted journalists to call him the "electrical wizard," an appellation he heartily disliked.

Though Steinmetz's inventions had none of the popular appeal of Edison's, he nevertheless solved hundreds of problems that had puzzled engineers for years, in the designing of transformers, motors, and generators, and the distribution of electricity for greater distances at higher voltage. It is generally recognized that the expansion of the electrical industry during the first two decades of the twentieth century

*The two papers on the mathematical law of magnetic hysteresis were hailed by contemporaries as doing for the magnetic circuit what the German physicist Georg Simon Ohm had done for the electric circuit.

was made possible by Steinmetz. Thus "a large share of the initial credit belongs to him for the progress made during his lifetime in the commercial application of electricity."[8]

The annual reports of the U.S. Patent Office from the turn of the century to 1923, the year Steinmetz died, contain repeated listings of his inventions. For 1900: "Steinmetz, Charles P., Schenectady, N.Y., assignor to General Electric Company. Regulation of dynamo-electric machines." In the same year he assigned to GE another invention, described as "a system of electrical distribution," and also a patent on "alternating current motive apparatus." There were eight Steinmetz patents that year alone, barely three years after he had gone to work for the company. The Patent Office listed Steinmetz's inventions almost every year. In 1910, for example, four inventions were recorded, each assigned to GE. A total of 195 patents were registered in Steinmetz's name. (Appropriation of an inventor's work by a corporate employer was, and continues to be, standard operating procedure.)

Steinmetz worked for GE for more than thirty years. The company built him a laboratory behind his Wendell Avenue home; he had free rein for his scientific projects, and GE was the technological and financial beneficiary of his genius. On many occasions he indicated that the relationship suited him, and that he found working for a large corporation preferable to employment by a small entrepreneur with limited means. In an article, "Socialism and Invention," he wrote:

> With the progress of the world's development towards organization into larger and larger corporations, steadily the number of independent engineers is decreasing, and more and more find it to their advantage to enter the employ of corporations. In corporation employment of the

> engineer, it is, however, to a large extent the custom that the inventions made by the engineer, and the patents covering them, belong to the company, and not to the inventor, and the inventor derives no direct financial benefit from his individual invention.[9]

Steinmetz did not complain about this arrangement. On the contrary, he justified it, pointing out:

> Usually the problem which the engineer solved by his invention had been brought before him by his work for the company, and the data and information which enabled him to solve the problem to a considerable extent was made available by the corporation. The engineer's compensation, then, is his pay, which covers the products of his knowledge as well as his originality and inventive skill.

Despite his advocacy of Socialism, Steinmetz's view of large corporations—and especially of General Electric—was most tolerant. He was bounded by his times and experiences, as well as by the relatively limited size and nature of the GE of his day. Marxists believe that the technical and industrial development of capitalism facilitates the transition to Socialism. Some Socialists, especially prior to World War I, mistakenly took this to mean that the corporate form assisted this transformation, and Steinmetz reflected this outlook.

Evidently viewing the corporation from the viewpoint of the elite, he wrote in his 1916 book *America and the New Epoch*:

> Of course the corporation organization is still crude and imperfect, and there are many chances to "get lost" or get into "blind-alley" positions.

> But, on the other hand, think of the positions of power, the big jobs that await the man of ability in large industrial corporations. And the man who gets into a blind-alley job does not have to stay there unless he wishes. If he has imagination enough to become discontented, he will soon move into a better job.*[10]

That he was aware of his exceptional status is suggested by his introduction to *America and the New Epoch*:

> When I landed at Castle Garden, from the steerage of a French liner, I had ten dollars and no job, and could speak no English. Now, personally, I have no fault to find with existing society; it has given me everything I wanted. I have been successful in professional engineering, and have every reason to be personally satisfied. The only criticism I can make is that I would far more enjoy my advantages if I knew that everybody else would enjoy the same. Fear must be allayed, the economic problem must be solved, and the worker must be relieved of worry over possible sickness, unemployment, and old age before his distinguishing human passion—creative achievement—can be expected to assert itself to any adequate degree.

Though gratified at his own good fortune, Steinmetz was mindful of "the disadvantaged," as they have since come to be called. He said in an article: "There is a Turkish proverb that

*For a comment on GE's paternalistic policy and union organization, see Appendix A.

the world belongs to the dissatisfied.... For me the one great underlying principle of all human progress is that 'divine discontent' which makes men strive for better conditions."[11]

General Electric was aware of the monetary value of their genius—Socialist or no Socialist. A GE brochure reviewed their chief consulting engineer's early years in Bismarck's Germany most sympathetically. It reported that as a young man Steinmetz had interests outside the university curriculum. These interests, the GE publication observed, "were to alter profoundly the current of his life." The brochure went on to say, "At this time, Bismarck was trying to stamp out Socialism in Germany; but with the enthusiasm of youth, a small company of students held secret meetings, and discussed social problems." Young Steinmetz joined this group despite police orders to arrest "all persons who would dare to question Bismarck's course."[12]

Steinmetz's entry into practical politics came with the election in 1911 of George R. Lunn as mayor of Schenectady on the Socialist ticket.[13] (Pro-Socialist sentiment had been growing in the country; Eugene V. Debs was to poll 901,000 votes the following year as a candidate for president of the United States.) Immediately upon assuming office, Lunn named Steinmetz to the city's Board of Education, which, in turn, elected him its president.

Always interested in children, Steinmetz found that only one school building had been erected during the prior four years, and it was in one of the more remote areas of the city. More than three thousand schoolchildren were without seats. When he assumed the presidency of the board, there were absolutely no facilities for retarded children. During his term of office, eight new schools were built, and special classes for retarded as well as tubercular children were established. Additional playgrounds were made available. Doctors and nurses became an integral part of the school system. In 1912, the board provided the first teacher for children with hearing problems.

Increasingly, Steinmetz encountered opposition from the Board of Estimate and Apportionment, which controlled the city's funds. In the next election—in 1913—he announced his candidacy for the presidency of the Common Council. Election would have assured him a vote on the Board of Estimate and Apportionment. Steinmetz and the entire Socialist Party ticket went down to defeat as the result of a fusion combination. Two years later, however, the electorate swung back to the Socialist administration. Steinmetz became president of the Common Council, although he had not made a single speech, or attended even one political mass meeting, or spent a cent on campaigning.

With the cooperation of the superintendent of schools, Dr. Abraham Brubacher, this is what Steinmetz accomplished:

- provided sufficient school accommodations so that there were no more half-time pupils;

- added thirty classrooms, and started building forty-six additional classrooms;

- arranged for medical examinations by a staff of seven full-time nurses and seven part-time physicians;

- introduced free textbooks in primary schools for all grades;

- established ungraded classes to deal with the English-language problems of foreign-born children;

- for the first time, created special classes in which retarded and tubercular children could get individual instruction;
- set up special classrooms for undernourished children, with three meals a day, under the supervision of school nurses.[14]

During World War I, in the winter of 1917–1918, Schenectady, along with many other American cities, experienced a severe fuel crisis. There was some sentiment in the Board of Education for closing the schools. Steinmetz opposed this move. No school would be shut down, he said, so long as a single place of public amusement remained open.

His educational philosophy is expressed in a statement made in 1921: "The teacher of the primary class is the most important person in the school system. Upon her understanding of the child, upon her capacity to arouse interest in the child mind, upon the nature of her first few guiding steps, the future career of the child largely rests."[15]

Steinmetz served on the Schenectady Common Council from 1916 to 1923, and on the Board of Education for three terms: from 1912 to 1914, 1916 to 1918, and 1922 to the time of his death the following year.

As the 1922 candidate of the Socialist and Farmer-Labor parties for state engineer and surveyor (then an elective office), he polled 291,000 votes, about half from New York City, and ran ahead of the ticket. In his campaign, he talked of harnessing Niagara, and the development of water power on the St. Lawrence, upper Hudson, and Delaware rivers.[16]

GE's benevolent attitude toward their chief consulting engineer apparently extended to the Schenectady Socialist administration. A contemporary student of Socialism in the

U.S. reports the experience of David I. Nelke, editor of the anti-Socialist Catholic publication the *Common Cause,* when he called on Charles A. Coffin, GE president, in 1912, one year after the Lunn administration had taken office. Nelke, seeking GE support for his magazine, had turned up at the suggestion of Ralph Easley of the "class peace" National Civic Federation. During a stormy session, Coffin attacked various statements in the *Common Cause* and said that "as far as he was concerned, Dr. Lunn was the best man who had ever been mayor of Schenectady."[17]

The Socialist administration that Steinmetz had joined in 1911 included twenty-three-year-old Walter Lippmann.[18] Recommended by the Socialist leader Morris Hillquit,[19] Lippmann became Mayor Lunn's executive assistant. He remained at his post only four months, however. He later wrote loftily, "To me it always seemed that we were like Peer Gynt struggling with the unwatered hinterland of the citizens of Schenectady."[20]

When he summarized his experiences in the Socialist *New York Call* he commented: "The Socialist Party was definitely hampered by the lack of men who combined professional training with Socialist vision.... There are plenty of people in this country bothering about playgrounds [a clear reference to Steinmetz's preoccupation with children]. These things are worth having, to be sure, but why not let the 'Progressives' do them?"[21]

Two months earlier, Lippmann's mood had been more sanguine. Writing in the *Masses*, he described the progress that was being made: "The Schenectady Health Department is preparing a system of records to follow the child from birth to the time he begins to earn a living. A maternity nurse has been appointed whose duty it is to teach expectant mothers the hygiene of the lying-in period and the care of the infant."[22]

Many years later, Lincoln Steffens, in a letter to his wife, Ella Winter, wrote: "I see that Walter Lippmann is back from his travels with Tom Lamont and is to have a column in the *Herald Tribune*. It will express Wall Street, I predict."[23] Sometime after Lippmann had begun writing his column, he received a congratulatory letter from William Allen White, editor of the *Emporia* (Kansas) *Gazette*, which concluded, "Don't let the Bankers get you!"[24]

As for Mayor Lunn, he eventually parted company with the Socialist Party, after the organization had opposed some of his appointments. When Lunn switched to the Democrats in 1916 near the end of his term and was elected to Congress, Steinmetz functioned as acting mayor for about ten months. Later, Lunn served as lieutenant-governor under Alfred E. Smith, and as a member of the New York State Public Service Commission. In 1920 he appeared as a "cooperative" witness before the notorious Lusk Committee, which had initiated expulsion proceedings against five legally elected Socialists in the New York State Legislature.[25]

From 1913 to 1917 Steinmetz was on the advisory council of the left-wing *New Review*. His associates on the council included Eugene V. Debs, Maxim Gorky, W. E. B. Du Bois, Gustavus Myers, and Mary Heaton Vorse. The contributors ranged from moderate and left-wing Socialists to syndicalists. A contemporary report has it that at the end of the first year of publication, the right wing, which dominated the New York Socialist organization, officially banned the sale or distribution of the *New Review* at their public meetings.

In an article in the magazine entitled "Russia the Real Menace," Steinmetz called for the defeat of tsarist Russia in the imperialist war of 1914–1918. He argued that a victory for the Romanovs would lead to the destruction "of all that Socialism has accomplished by a submergency under an autocracy based on the illiterate masses."[26] Another article by Steinmetz was apparently rejected by the editors of the *New Review.* This article discussed the sinking of the British liner *Lusitania* on March 7, 1915, off the Irish coast by a German submarine, with a loss of 1,195 passengers and crew, including 128 Americans. A warning to U.S. citizens taking passage on British vessels, signed "Imperial German Embassy," had appeared in the American press the morning the ship was scheduled to sail. The U.S. had not yet entered the conflict, and the episode created intense pro-war fever.

That Steinmetz had been asked to contribute to the *New Review* symposium on the *Lusitania*[27] is suggested by a copy of the article, "The Sinking of the *Lusitania*,"* which I found among the Van Vechten Papers in Schenectady with Steinmetz's notation, "For the *New Review*—not used."[28]

The sinking of the ship, Steinmetz wrote, was "a horrible atrocity." However, those who traveled on the ship "did so with their eyes open, and of their own free will." He termed the *Lusitania* "an ammunition carrier." Subsequent research has confirmed his assessment. A 1975 study states that the overwhelming bulk of the freight consisted of munitions: "Many neutral onlookers believed that the *Lusitania* was in effect an auxiliary cruiser of the British Admiralty."[29] A British television documentary, "The Sinking of the *Lusitania*," presents similar evidence.

*For the text of the article, see Appendix B.

Addressing fifteen thousand farmers at the convention of the Non-Partisan League, in St. Paul, Minnesota, on September 20, 1917, Senator Robert M. La Follette, Sr., of Wisconsin was explaining why he had opposed America's entry into the war, when someone asked, "What about the *Lusitania*?" He replied:

> Four days before the *Lusitania* was to sail, President Wilson was warned in person by Secretary of State Bryan that the *Lusitania* had six million pounds of ammunition on board, besides explosives, and that the passengers who proposed to sail on that vessel were sailing in violation of a statute of this country that no passenger shall travel on a railroad train or on a vessel which carries dangerous explosives. And Secretary Bryan appealed to President Wilson to stop passengers from sailing on the *Lusitania*. I am giving you some history that probably has not been given you before.[30]

Despite his reputation as an outspoken radical, Steinmetz was a popular speaker even during World War I, when he was often accused of "pro-Germanism" in the jingo press. In a three-column account of a lecture given in Fort Wayne, Indiana, the local newspaper reported that the city "had felt highly honored by the coming of this mastermind in the electrical world." Steinmetz was quoted as saying, in words that only now are commonly uttered:

> We have been a wasteful nation because of our great natural wealth. Nothing has been saved. We have lived in the today and never thought, nor prepared, for tomorrow. What have we been

> doing for years? We have been destroying our forests to get lumber in the most extravagant way. We have taken out crops year after year and never put anything back in the earth. There has been no such thing as conservation. It has been destruction.[31]

The press-clipping file preserved for years by Steinmetz's secretary, friends, and associates discloses a wide response to his assertion in late 1922—when U.S. labor was experiencing a furious anti-union assault—that modern technology was capable of providing a universal four-hour day. All that was necessary, he said, was the elimination of waste in our present industrial system:

> You encounter waste everywhere. Two similar stores on opposite corners. Large sales organizations putting in long hours developing artificial needs. Factories working nights to supply things that must be sold instead of bought. Shipyards turning out battleships whose only purpose is destruction. Waste and duplication of effort all around us.[32]

Steinmetz followed events in Soviet Russia with rapt and sympathetic interest. On February 16, 1922, he wrote to V. I. Lenin, offering his assistance in the electrification program then under way. Because of the unreliability of mail service between the United States and Soviet Russia, Steinmetz sent his letter via B. V. Losev, secretary of the New York branch of the Russian Technical Aid Society, who was returning to his homeland. When the scientist entrusted his letter to Losev, he observed: "It is a pity I cannot go with you.... Let them know in Russia that I and many others sympathize with their aims, and that we are with them with all our hearts and minds." Here is what Steinmetz wrote:

> Dear Mr. Lenin:
>
> Mr. B. V. Losev's return to Russia gives me the opportunity to express to you my admiration of the wonderful work of social and industrial regeneration which Russia is accomplishing under such terrible difficulties. I wish you the fullest success, and have every confidence that you will succeed. Indeed, you must succeed, for the great work which Russia has started must not be allowed to fail.
>
> If in technical and more particularly in electrical engineering matters I can assist Russia in any manner with advice, suggestions, or consultation, I shall always be very pleased to do so as far as I am able.
>
> Fraternally yours,
> Charles Steinmetz[33]

Lenin received Steinmetz's message on March 31, 1922. On April 10, he replied:

> Dear Dr. Steinmetz:
>
> I thank you cordially for your friendly letter of February 16, 1922. I must admit to my shame that I heard your name for the first time only a few months ago from Comrade Krzhizhanovsky, who was chairman of our State Commission for Working Out a Plan for the Electrification of Russia and is now chairman of the State General Planning Commission.[34] He told me of the out-

standing position which you have gained among the electrical engineers of the whole world.

Comrade Martens has now made me better acquainted by his accounts of you.[35] I have seen from these accounts that your sympathies with Soviet Russia have been aroused, on the one hand, by your social and political views. On the other hand, as a representative of electrical engineering, and particularly in one of the technically advanced countries, you have become convinced of the necessity and inevitability of the replacement of capitalism by a new social order, which will establish the planned regulation of economy and ensure the welfare of the entire mass of the people on the basis of the electrification of entire countries. In all countries of the world there is growing—more slowly than one would like, but irresistibly and unswervingly—the number of representatives of science, technology, art who are becoming convinced of the necessity of replacing capitalism by a different socio-economic system, and whom the "terrible difficulties"* of the struggle of Soviet Russia against the capitalist world do not repel, do not frighten away, but, on the contrary, lead to an understanding of the inevitability of the struggle and the necessity of taking what part in it they can, helping the new to overcome the old.

In particular, I want to thank you for your offer to help Russia with your advice, suggestions,

*These two words were written by Lenin in English.

> etc. As the absence of officially and legally recognized relations between Soviet Russia and the United States makes the practical realization of your offer extremely difficult both for us and for you, I will allow myself to publish both your letter and my reply in the hope that many persons who live in America, or in countries connected by commercial treaties with the United States and Russia, will then help you (by information, by translations from Russian into English, etc.) to give effect to your intention of helping the Soviet Republic.
>
> With very best greetings,
>
> Yours fraternally,
> Lenin[36]

In underscoring his support for the Soviet electrification program, Steinmetz obliquely indicted a system whereby the burgeoning electrical industry in the U.S. was highly profitable while, ironically, millions of American homes and farmsteads were without electric power. When he made his offer to Lenin, the American scientist was aware of the crucial importance of electrification in industrializing Soviet Russia. "Anyone who has carefully observed life in the countryside, as compared with life in the cities," Lenin had declared in 1920, "knows that we have not torn up the roots of capitalism and have not undermined the foundation, the basis, of the internal enemy. The latter depends on small-scale production, and there is only one way of undermining it, namely to place the economy of the country, including agriculture, on a new technical basis, that of modern, large-scale production. Only electricity provides that basis." Steinmetz was undoubtedly aware of Lenin's slogan "Communism is Soviet power plus the electrification of the whole country." If this aim were not accomplished, Lenin pointed out, Russia would remain a small peasant country. "Only when the country has been electrified, and industry, agriculture, and transport have been placed on the technical basis of modern large-scale industry, only then shall we be fully victorious," the Soviet leader said in his report on the activities of the Council of People's Commissars to the Eighth All-Russian Congress of Soviets on December 22, 1920.[37]

Lenin continued his correspondence with Steinmetz. A few months after he had sent his first letter in response to the American scientist's offer of assistance, the Soviet leader wrote again. This letter, however, was not mailed. Instead, it was entrusted to Harold M. Ware, an American agronomist, who was returning to the United States.[38] On the back of a photograph of himself, Lenin wrote:

> To the highly esteemed Charles Proteus Steinmetz, one of the few exceptions to the united front of representatives of science and culture opposed to the proletariat. I hope that a further deepening and widening of the breach in the front will not have to be awaited long. Let the example of the Russian workers and peasants, holding their fate in their own hands, serve as an encouragement to the American proletariat and farmers. In spite of the terrible consequences of war destruction, we are going ahead, though not possessing to the extent of one-tenth the tremendous resources for the economic building of a new life that have been at the disposal of the American people for many years.[39]

Describing his meeting with Steinmetz in Schenectady, Ware wrote that the scientist "was tremendously pleased with the picture and the expression of comradeship it carried." Ware reported that Steinmetz at once "began to probe me for first-hand information on Russia." When Ware said his experience was largely among the peasants, Steinmetz replied that that was precisely what he was interested in. "There is no reason why Russia cannot carry out her electrification slowly," he told Ware, "but I hope America, Germany, etc., will help."[40] Steinmetz placed Lenin's photograph on the wall of his GE laboratory, and he proudly pointed it out to both sympathetic and unsympathetic visitors.

There is a rather engaging sidelight on Lenin's initial response to Steinmetz's offer of assistance. On the day that he received the scientist's letter, Lenin turned it over to G. M. Krzhizhanovsky, chief of the State Commission for Electrification, with this message:

> I enclose what I have received today. I remember you telling me about Steinmetz that he is a world figure. Before you told me about him I had never heard his name.... Shouldn't I make some practical proposition in my reply? After all, he has offered his assistance. In view of this, shouldn't I specify some *concrete* types of assistance? Have all the works on electrification been sent to him? Do you think it worth publishing his letter and my reply? Please return the enclosure and this letter with your advice. I think I should also consult Martens. We must give more thought to the best way of replying.
>
> Yours,
> Lenin[41]

Jessica Smith has written in *New World Review* that Lenin's first letter had not reached Steinmetz, and it was Harold Ware who brought a duplicate copy to the scientist's laboratory in Schenectady. In her account, she notes that Steinmetz did receive reports of the State Commission for Electrification from Lenin. On the basis of these reports, Steinmetz described the Soviet electrification plan in the September 30, 1922, issue of *Electrical World*, and he concluded the article with an appeal for American aid in carrying out the program.[42]

Describing Fred Biedenkapp's speaking tour on behalf of Russian orphans, the magazine *Soviet Russia* reported that while in Schenectady he had sold ten shares of stock of the Russian-American Industrial Corporation,[43] at ten dollars a share, to "Charles P. Steinmetz, the internationally known inventor, who took the occasion to endorse the work done toward the reconstruction of Russia's economy."[44]

One of the fascinating, hitherto-unpublished documents that I found in Schenectady was a letter from Harold Ware, dated August 4, 1923, barely three months before Steinmetz's death.* Ware was seeking Steinmetz's help with a project whose aim was to interest American industrialists in selling Soviet Russia tractors on credit. The plan, as described by Ware, had been worked out in cooperation with Frank P. Walsh, a prominent Kansas City, Missouri, attorney who had served as chairman of the U.S. Commission on Industrial Relations from 1913 to 1915.

Early in July 1923, Steinmetz had agreed to join an advisory committee to aid the Kuzbas mining colony in Siberia.[45] Other Americans on the committee were James H. Maurer,

*For the text of Ware's letter, see Appendix C.

president of the Pennsylvania State Federation of Labor;[46] Walter N. Polakov, economist; and Roger N. Baldwin of the American Civil Liberties Bureau (later the American Civil Liberties Union). The *New York Times* was accurate in its statement that the Kuzbas colony consisted of five hundred Americans, but it incorrectly reported that the group was operating under "a valuable coal mining concession."[47]

A number of Americans in the colony had broken their two-year contracts and returned home. Writing from Kemerovo, Siberia, Ruth Epperson Kennell reported that some had become disillusioned because "they came with misconceptions of the project, gained from inaccurate information." Others, she wrote, had arrived "with sentimental illusions concerning our importance in Russia."[48]

It was in response to a concerted press campaign aimed at discrediting the Kuzbas experiment that Steinmetz accepted membership on its advisory committee. He wrote:

> I am very much interested in Kuzbas and hope much from it. Everybody taking an interest in the enterprise knows, or should know, that it is the creation of a better world in which he is taking part, but that he goes out into a field where he must expect hardships and disappointments, and where he must organize and create. There are always a few people who imagine that in such an enterprise they will drop into a safe berth and have a good and easy time, and then get disappointed and come back and throw mud after they have met reality.[49]

Steinmetz also served on the editorial board of *Soviet Russia Pictorial*, along with William Z. Foster, Ella Reeve

Bloor, Upton Sinclair, J. Louis Engdahl, Henry Wadsworth Longfellow Dana, Elizabeth Gurley Flynn, Paxton Hibben, Helen Keller, Albert Rhys Williams, and Mary Heaton Vorse. The official organ of the Friends of Soviet Russia and the International Committee for Workers' Aid (later Workers' International Relief), it told the story of Soviet Russia's progress, as well as its problems, and raised funds to aid the victims of the famine along the Volga in the twenties. One issue of the magazine acknowledged a contribution of $140 from Steinmetz; $18 from the Socialist leader Eugene V. Debs, convalescing in a sanatorium in Elmhurst, Illinois; and $28 from the famous classical singer Alma Gluck.[50]

Because of his correspondence with Lenin, Steinmetz incurred the displeasure of one of the early red-baiters. In a curious mélange titled *Reds in America* (1924), the author, R. M. Whitney, after noting that Steinmetz "had for many years been known as an enthusiastic intellectual Socialist," proclaimed:

> Whenever a college professor, a government official, a big businessman, or any individual whose name carries distinction in any line of endeavor, expresses an opinion that can be construed as favoring, even in a limited sense, the aims of the Communists, such words are seized upon and used for propaganda purposes.... Thus it is that the correspondence between ... Charles P. Steinmetz, the electrical genius, and Lenin was broadcasted throughout the English-speaking world and was translated in many languages. It was given out by Lenin.[51]

An early biographer, also commenting on the Lenin-Steinmetz correspondence, was more amiable. But while the lyrics were different, the music was the same. "The incident," wrote J. W. Hammond, "did not add to the prestige of Dr. Steinmetz in the opinion of many persons who fail to sympathize with the Soviet point of view. They were quick to criticize his action, which led them to consider Steinmetz as more of a visionary than a practical idealist, and in any event a man whose political and social views were far from safe." Hammond observed dolefully, "Yet Dr. Steinmetz quietly continued his interest in Russia and Russian events to the very last." As evidence, Hammond cited the fact that Steinmetz had contributed $250 he received for a magazine article toward the purchase of tractors for Soviet agricultural development.[52]

That Steinmetz's interest in the progress of Soviet reconstruction was not ephemeral is attested to by his introduction to A. A. Heller's book *The Industrial Revival in Soviet Russia*,[53] published the same year in which he had written to Lenin.[54] Political democracy, Steinmetz noted, has not solved the social problem, "and never will."

> The first scientific approach to the problem is the work of Marx, half a century ago..... Socialism is a society free from unsocial acts, thus is identical with that of Christianity as taught by Jesus. The difference is that Christianity endeavored to bring about this condition by inculcating brotherly love into all members of human society, and the experience of nineteen centuries has proven that self-interest is stronger than brotherly love. Socialism abandons the hope of changing human nature and eliminates unsocial acts by reorganiz-

> ing society so that self-interest becomes identical with public interest, that is, by eliminating those conditions under which self-interest is opposed to public interest.

Commenting on the years immediately following the Bolshevik Revolution, Steinmetz's words are prescient in light of subsequent events: "There was no previous experience to guide; nobody could foresee many of the happenings, and much which was done had to be done over again, might have been done differently, if the future could have been known."

In addition to books and articles on scientific subjects, Steinmetz wrote for both the popular, mass-circulation magazines, from which he received fees, and the Socialist and labor press, from which he neither sought nor expected any payment. His byline appeared frequently in *Collier's*, *Harper's*, the *American*, the *Review of Reviews*, *Good Housekeeping*, the *Survey*, the *Ladies' Home Journal*, and the *Nation*, as well as the left-wing *New Review* and the Socialist *New York Call*. He often addressed letters to editors of newspapers in Schenectady and Albany, and they were always featured. Most of these communications dealt not with electrical engineering but with current social and political issues.

Steinmetz's interests outside of the scientific field were boundless: history, literature, photography, gardening, boating, nature study, motoring, and cycling. He liked best the picturesque ride on the old roads to Lake George, sixty-five miles from Schenectady. Perhaps above all, as city historian Larry Hart has written, Steinmetz loved the frequent excursions to his unpretentious camp on Viele's Creek, a tributary of the Mohawk River not far from his home. Much of his technical work was done there, while he was either drifting alone in a canoe or seated cross-legged before the rough plank table on the porch of his shack.*

One day, on a train to Salt Lake City, Steinmetz heard a tap on his compartment door. The visitor was William Jennings Bryan, a frequent candidate for president of the United States and a much-publicized Fundamentalist. The meeting was most cordial, despite the two men's sharply opposing views on religion. Anticipating Clarence Darrow's famous joust with Bryan at the "monkey trial" (Dayton, Tennessee, 1925), Steinmetz told Bryan that he could not believe anything he could not prove. His scientific training and mode of thinking, he said, had made this imperative.

On another occasion, in a talk to a church audience in Schenectady, Steinmetz asserted: "There is no evidence outside of science for God, immortality, and similar conceptions. There is evidence against these conceptions in science, and science has justified its methods and conclusions by the work it has done."[55]

Not long after his arrival in Schenectady, Steinmetz was invited to join the faculty of Union College, where he served as professor of electrical engineering and electrophysics from 1902 to 1923. (The college later awarded him an honorary Ph.D., and there is a Steinmetz Hall at Union.) Steinmetz divided his time between the college and his GE laboratory. His large red-brick home near the college was surrounded by wide lawns and a bit of woodland. Behind the house was the scientist's private laboratory and a glass conservatory where he grew orchids and other exotic plants.

*The camp was dismantled in 1930 and was moved to Henry Ford's museum of Americana in Dearborn, Michigan, where it was reassembled.

Steinmetz never married. He legally adopted as his son and heir a young engineer, J. LeRoy Hayden.* When Hayden married Corinne Rost, the young couple made their home with Steinmetz. The children born to the Haydens—Joseph, Margaret, and William—became Steinmetz's foster grandchildren. To all of them, including Mr. and Mrs. Hayden, he was "Daddy," as he always signed his letters and postcards to them when on lecture tours.

Although he owned two electrically-powered automobiles, Steinmetz preferred to board "the workmen's trolley" at Rugby Road and Wendell Avenue, which took him straight to GE's main gate.

Interviewed by a reporter for a Michigan newspaper, he listed among his favorite books Homer's *Odyssey*, Johann Wolfgang von Goethe's *Faust*, Horace's *Odes* and his other poetry, Robert Louis Stevenson's *Treasure Island*, Mark Twain's *The Adventures of Tom Sawyer* and *The Adventures of Huckleberry Finn*, and Theodor Mommsen's *History of Rome.*

He liked to cook and knew how to prepare a good meal. This skill became widely known, and one day he received a letter from a New Yorker requesting his recipe for meat loaf. The scientist responded with a detailed letter providing it.†

There are countless stories about Steinmetz, many of them untrue. The most popular and persistent is that he once refused to work in his laboratory because of a "No Smoking" sign. According to legend, he quietly departed, saying only, "No smoking, no Steinmetz." Some light is cast on the "no smoking" issue by August Claessens, a well-known Socialist

*He died on August 12, 1951, at the age of seventy.

†For the text of this letter, see Appendix D.

propagandist of the time and former New York State assemblyman, who had visited him in Schenectady.

"All around the laboratory I saw signs, 'No Smoking,'" Claessens recalled in his autobiography. Seeing the scientist puffing away at one of his favorite Blackstone panatellas, Claessens politely sought an explanation. "Steinmetz took out his cigar for a moment and whispered to me, 'You see, my good comrade, my boss is understanding: "No smoking, no inventing."'"[56]

Finding it difficult to take notes fast enough as a student in Breslau, Steinmetz had developed his own system of shorthand, which he used throughout his life. The method is a blend of several systems, chiefly the Swedish Arenda, with modifications that he had devised. Its underlying principle is phonetic. After he had been using the method for a number of years he offered it for publication as a book to Harper and Brothers. Four years earlier they had published *America and the New Epoch.* The manuscript was rejected on August 10, 1920, in a letter that bore no signature, only the name of the firm: "The general opinion seems to be that your system is difficult to master, and that while it might be readily understood and acquired by people of superior intelligence, it would on that account hardly appeal to the general public, upon which we have to depend for a large sale."

On September 1, 1923, Steinmetz began a trip to California. He had been invited to deliver the keynote address at the Pacific Coast convention of the American Institute of Electrical Engineers, in Del Monte, California. (The Haydens traveled with him, at his suggestion.) Along the return route he lectured before scientific groups in various cities. The trip proved more taxing than either he or members of his family had anticipated. Soon after reaching home on October 13, 1923, he fell ill. He was ordered to bed, but his doctors said that his condition was not serious. The *New York Times* headlined its story "Dr. Steinmetz Just Resting":

> There is no need for alarm over the condition of Dr. Charles Steinmetz, the inventor's physician announced this morning, denying the authenticity of reports that Dr. Steinmetz is ill. The physician said he is but resting up in bed after a somewhat too strenuous trip to the Pacific Coast. The doctor said that the only difficulty was to keep the patient in bed, Dr. Steinmetz being anxious to get up and go about perfecting his present pet project—development of generators of man-made lightning.[57]

But despite this optimistic prognosis, Steinmetz died four days later. He was fifty-eight years old. A local newspaper reported:

> Death came suddenly today to Charles Proteus Steinmetz, the "wizard" of electricity, while he was alone in his sickroom, which he was counting on leaving soon, so far had his recovery progressed. The scientist slept most soundly last night of any night since the breakdown which sent him to bed following his recent trip to the Pacific Coast. He asked his nurse to have his breakfast served to him in bed, and she left the room to have the meal prepared. William Hayden, one of his adopted grandchildren, entered the room a short time after eight o'clock with the breakfast and found the scientist dead.

His physicians issued this bulletin: "Dr. Steinmetz died suddenly a few minutes after eight o'clock this morning of acute dilation of the heart, following a chronic myocarditis of many years' standing, which is a weakening of the heart muscles." The same newspaper in which the medical bulletin appeared told its readers that, despite rumors that Steinmetz had received one of the highest salaries ever paid to an electrical expert, "his friends say he left a very modest fortune. In fact, it was said that he was not on the payroll of General Electric, but that the company paid all of his living expenses and those of his experiments. He held that sufficient."[58]

A *New York Times* dispatch from Schenectady reported that the only insurance Steinmetz carried was a policy for $1,500 provided by GE and that the principal sum would be paid to his half-sister Clara. This was in addition to $1,000 to a younger half-sister, Margarethe Machie of Breslau, "if she be living." Contrary to tales about the scientist's fabulous salary, probate of his will disclosed that the estate was not sufficient to cover bequests totaling $25,500.[59]

Steinmetz's death was marked by solemn but simple rites. The service was conducted by an old friend, Reverend Ernest Caldecott, pastor of the Unitarian Church of Schenectady. Steinmetz's half-sister Clara, his adopted son, LeRoy Hayden, and his family, and a few intimate friends attended the half-hour service in the Wendell Avenue home, while outside five hundred gathered. City schools and Union College were closed for the day; city and county offices and many business establishments were shut down for half a day.

For four hours, unbroken lines of people filed past the bier as it lay in a flower-filled room of the Steinmetz home. Representatives from the city government, the schools, Union College, and several industries, as well as groups of children, came to pay homage to a man known internationally for his development of electrical energy, and locally as "a good citizen," as the *Times* put it.[60] At Vale Cemetery more than fifteen hundred gathered to pay their final respects. Honorary pallbearers included Owen D. Young, chairman of the board of General Electric; Gerard Swope, president of GE; and Dr. Charles A. Richmond, president of Union College.

An eloquent tribute was offered by a fellow scientist and Socialist, Professor Vladimir Karapetoff of the Cornell University School of Electrical Engineering.[61] Steinmetz, he wrote in the *Cornell Daily Sun*, belonged to a political party that "cussed his company, GE, and its principal customers for years." Karapetoff recalled Steinmetz as "modest, thoughtful, a prodigious worker....His contribution to our welfare and our knowledge is beyond measure or computation, and his life is a shining example of a quiet, straight, and unswerving path amidst the turmoil of conflicting positions, avarice, pseudo-science, pseudo-patriotism, and pseudo-life itself."[62]

Those critics of contemporary capitalist society who have achieved eminence in their chosen fields are frequently the targets of ideological adversaries who seek to explain away their advanced social views as something alien to their "true calling." Thus, following Steinmetz's death, the *New York Times* proclaimed, "As an engineer, Steinmetz started with a thorough training, while as a publicist and economist, he had none at all."[63] This appraisal is refuted by the obituary on Steinmetz that had appeared in the very same newspaper five days earlier. There, *Times* readers were informed that, in addition to his studies of mathematics, chemistry, and electrical engineering, Steinmetz "was deeply interested in politics and economics and became an active Socialist at a time when the German government under Bismarck was taking drastic steps to stamp out Socialism." The obituary also noted that Steinmetz had been a leader of several Socialist clubs and editor of Socialist publications.[64]

Some years after Steinmetz's death, Governor Herbert Lehman signed a bill establishing his residence as an historic site. In 1938, however, after much wrangling in the New York State Legislature over the needed appropriations, the home was torn down. A simple marker is all that remains today.

Newspaper writers had placed Steinmetz's annual earnings at somewhere between $25,000 and $100,000. However, when I interviewed the scientist's foster grandson Joseph Hayden in 1976, he said he doubted that the figure ever exceeded $25,000, "if that." Taking time out from work in his photocopy shop near the Schenectady bus station, he spoke of Steinmetz's great love for children and his special devotion to his foster grandchildren. "The Doctor wanted very much for me to become an electrical engineer, but I just couldn't make it at Union. When I changed my major, I saw that he couldn't hide his disappointment. He was always very patient and understanding, as well as entertaining. When we were kids, he used to drop everything he was doing, even interrupting a visit with old Henry Ford once, to tell us a bedtime story. We accompanied him to his camp on weekends, where he cooked all the meals and we set the table and washed the dishes. He always found time to help us with our homework. People from all walks of life were always amazed at how he could discuss *anything*."[65]

Joseph Hayden's sister, Margaret, interviewed by *GE News* forty years after Steinmetz's death, said, "I remember that he had a firm conviction that everyone should be treated with respect and kindness." Racial and ethnic slurs "were bandied about on the playground at school, but the first time I tried one of these at home, my grandfather scolded me severely and explained that such talk was disrespectful, and furthermore, it might hurt someone."[66]

Celia Rhein was Steinmetz's last secretary, and she was approaching her ninety-fifth birthday when we talked about the great scientist and social thinker in her modest apartment in a working-class section of Schenectady. When she learned that she might become Steinmetz's secretary, she was a bit apprehensive: "I expected to see a tall, imposing, forbidding individual. Instead, there was this very kindly little man who later proved to be so thoughtful and considerate, not only of me, but of all the people with whom he came in contact."

The only condition that Steinmetz set for her employment, she said, was that she master the personal system of shorthand in which he wrote his notes: "I began studying his system and quickly learned it. In the margins of letters that Steinmetz wanted answered, he would often write this instruction: 'Write a nice letter, not too long, not too short.' He used to say, 'All I want is good work; never sacrifice accuracy for speed.' He always said, 'What's new?' when he came through the door each morning."[66] (Interviewed years earlier by Larry Hart, Miss Rhein had told how Steinmetz was "always neat in his attire; he wore gray suits and often a turtleneck sweater. His hair was cut in semi-brush style, his beard always carefully trimmed.") Because of his deformity, Miss Rhein explained, Steinmetz seldom used the expensive leather chair that GE had provided. He preferred instead to kneel on a chair or stool when working. The floor of his laboratory was never waxed, she said, because of the danger that he might slip and injure himself.

"When the Doctor died, GE wanted to dispose of all the newspaper clippings about him that I had collected and arranged in chronological order. No space, they said. So I asked if I could take the clippings away, and they agreed. I put them in cartons and kept them under my uncle's upright piano for more than thirty years."[67] (The clippings are now in the Schenectady City History Center and the Research Library of the Schenectady County Historical Society.)

Several weeks after I had interviewed her, remembering that it was her ninety-fifth birthday, I telephoned Miss Rhein from New York to offer my congratulations. We chatted again about her boss, and about the razing of the Steinmetz home, and how it could have served as a facility for the elderly. "Not for me," she hastened to say, "but for those who need such a place more than I. The Doctor had such a beautiful greenhouse, with orchids, and now everything is overgrown with weeds. It's really a shame."[68]

Many have visited Steinmetz's burial place. A photo in an Albany newspaper showed Eugene V. Debs placing a wreath on the grave. The caption under the picture described Debs as "a personal friend" of Steinmetz's.[69]

On December 31, 1923, two months after Steinmetz's death, General Electric issued its annual report.[70] In the "Condensed Profit and Loss Account," the company informed its stockholders of how business had been during fiscal 1923; it hadn't been at all bad: "Net sales billed—$271,309,695.37; profit available for dividends—$33,525,118.32; surplus at December 31, 1923—$82,762,095.65." But the stockholders had to be told about one other aspect of corporate affairs: "Dr. Charles P. Steinmetz died on October 26, 1923, after thirty years of devoted service with your company."[71]

Appendix A

GE's Paternalistic Policy and Union Organization

The possibility of "moving into a better job," as Steinmetz put it, doubtless applied to him and other gifted scientists who were economically valuable to their employers, but not to the average employee at GE. It is worth noting that Local 301 of the United Electrical, Radio, and Machine Workers (UE) did not win collective bargaining rights in Schenectady until December 16, 1936, although thirty craft locals organized in the Electrical Industry Trades Alliance had negotiated with GE with varying success in previous years.

UE leader James Matles (1909–1975), in discussing the company's paternalistic policy as reflected in its "labor code" (GE Q105A), conceded that the code outlined issues spelled out in a union contract: it set forth prevailing GE policies on wages, hours, overtime, vacations, and employment conditions in the shop. The code also declared, "There shall be no discrimination by foremen, superintendents, or any executives of the company against any employee because of race or creed or because of an employee's membership in any fraternity, society, or labor or other organization."

Steinmetz, Matles pointed out, "could be a Socialist or anything 'lawful' that he pleased. As long as he was valuable to GE—his genius made millions for the company—he would be kept on the job. The no-discrimination clause in GE's Q105A established the same principle for all employees."[72]

During the McCarthy era, however, GE management actively joined in driving from their jobs scores of employees with many years of service. These trade unionists had invoked the protection of the Bill of Rights of the U.S. Constitution and had refused to submit to the inquisitors.

Appendix B

The Sinking of the *Lusitania* by Charles P. Steinmetz*

It was a horrible atrocity, just as horrible as every act of war, and far worse horrors have occurred, and are occurring daily in the trenches and on the battlefield, without causing a ripple in public sentiment. Some horrors will continue and increase until war is swept out of existence by a reorganization of society which makes war useless and thereby unnecessary.

These passengers [who] embarked on the ammunition carrier *Lusitania* did so with their eyes open, after repeated warnings and of their own free will, but those tens of thousands of Russians [who] slowly sank to death in the mire of the Masurian Lakes, those English, Germans, French who daily are slaughtered in the trenches, are there not by their free will but by military law, or have been forced to "voluntarily" enlist to escape starvation by unemployment.

Hundreds of thousands of innocent women and children have starved to death on the plains of Poland without stirring the sentiment of the humanitarians. What, then, is the difference? Amongst those who went down in the *Lusitania* were some of America's highest nobility, and if the submarine blockade should become fully effective and stop our

*Unpublished article prepared for the *New Review*.

commerce with England, it would be a severe blow to America's most profitable business of manufacturing supplies and ammunition.

Schenectady, N.Y.
May 18, 1915

Appendix C

Letter from Harold M. Ware to Charles P. Steinmetz

41 Washington Square South,
New York City
August 4, 1923

Mr. Charles P. Steinmetz
Schenectady, New York

Dear Mr. Steinmetz:

Last Spring, when I delivered Comrade Lenin's letter and photograph to you, I told you that I was interested in developing tractor farming in Russia. Since then I have made a trip through the agricultural states from North Dakota to the Gulf, and subsequently a trip to the larger tractor manufacturers for the All-Russian Agricultural Exhibition now being held in Moscow. These contacts, plus my Russian experiences, are the basis of the proposed plan which was worked out with Frank P. Walsh.

My Russian experience taught me this: (a) that tractors are essential to the reconstruction of Russian agriculture, but a demand from the Russian farmers themselves must be created; (b) that the work we started at Perm of teaching

Russians to operate them is the only sound plan; we must measure our success by the rapidity with which Russians replace Americans, not only in operation of machinery, but in management of large-scale farming fitted to American machinery; (c) that Russia has no money to finance these educational farms and that the relief organizations are unsuited to the task; (d) that whatever plan is followed, it must be put on an economic basis, paving the way and affording inducements to American capitalist manufacturers to advance the essential CREDIT; (e) lastly, it cannot succeed without an initial nucleus of young, strong, and expert tractor farmers and mechanics with trained agricultural direction. And some responsibility and compensation must be offered to them. The unit which I took to Russia, with a few additions, fills these personal requirements. A representative of the group visited the Ukraine and in conversations with the officials quoted was assured that they would cooperate.

The American manufacturer is "from Missouri," i.e., they want to see the tangible "red seal," etc. Some of their representatives are in Moscow at the Agricultural Exhibition; all are anxious for business and all are timid about starting. In order to get a definite offer I am going back to Russia this month, probably on the 18th.

You said you were interested in the peasantry, in anything which affected them as important to the continuation of the Russian experiment as a whole. I feel that every tractor put into operation becomes a tremendous force to that end. And every Russian soldier and peasant taught to operate a tractor becomes, by the mere preaching of the gospel of tractor-farming in the villages, a factor in revolutionizing agriculture. Which, after all, is the ultimate stage of the Revolution.

Comrade Lenin was good enough to compliment the boys on their work at Perm last year. Most of them are participating in this project. They have little money, but their experience wore off the edge of adventure which drew them originally to Russia, and they have continued because they felt that they were doing valuable and constructive work for the first time in their lives.

Any help that you can give us will be invaluable. I would appreciate any criticism and suggestions you make upon the plan that would tend to make it more palatable to the American capitalist. Also, if you have any message you would like delivered personally in Moscow, I am at your service.

Cordially yours,
Harold M. Ware

Appendix D

Steinmetz's Recipe for Meat Loaf

Schenectady
July 17, 1922

Mr. C. M. Sheridan
No. 2 Gramercy Park,
New York City

Dear Sir:

I have been consulted about very many things, but yours is the first time I have been consulted on gastronomical matters. As for your second letter, it follows that you really want a cooking recipe. I give you herewith from my camping experience the following favorite dish of mine.

Meat Loaf

> Beef, veal, and pork (sirloin steak and chops), 1/2 lb. each. Cut off the bones and the fat from the beef and veal, leaving the fat on the pork. Then pass all three through the meat grinder, chopping it fairly fine. Add two complete raw eggs and finely sliced bacon (Beechnut bacon, cut

in pieces about 1 sq. in.) and mix everything thoroughly together, adding the proper amount of salt and if available celery salt. Form into the shape of a round loaf. In a cast iron or cast aluminum frying pan (that is, a pan of sufficiently heavy metal to well distribute the heat and guard against local burning) melt some butter, then put the meat loaf in the melted butter, cover the pan, and heat on a very low fire, turning over after some time, and continue for a long time, until very throughly cooked through. Add butter once or twice, when absorbed. Then uncover and greatly raise the fire, turning over after a little while, until well browned on both sides. Then take the meat loaf, put on a warm platter or plate, and pour a cup of cream or good milk into the pan. Stir until the sediment in the pan is dissolved, and heat until you get a good brown gravy. Pour this over the meat loaf and serve with boiled mealy potatoes. What is left over can be eaten cold, sliced, and served on buttered bread or toast.

Yours very truly,
Charles P. Steinmetz

William Dean Howells and the Haymarket Era

> For many weeks, for months, it has not been for one hour out of my waking thoughts; it is the last thing when I lie down, and the first thing when I rise up. It blackens my life. I feel the horror and the shame of the crime which the law is about to commit against justice.

These anguished words were written to a friend by William Dean Howells, the foremost American literary figure of his time, shortly before the hanging of the Haymarket martyrs on November 11, 1887.

They are buried under an impressive monument at Waldheim Cemetery in Forest Hill Park, in Chicago. August Spies was indeed prophetic when he said on the scaffold, "There will come a time when our silence will be more powerful than the voices you strangle today."[1]

Not long after the executions in the Cook County Jail, in Chicago, Howells received a letter from London. Enclosed were "one or two" short stories by a Norwegian author that the writer of the letter had translated into English. She said:

> I take the liberty of sending you the translations because ever since you had the courage to sign the appeal demanding a new trial for the Anarchists I have known you were not only a true artist and a great writer, but that even rarer thing, a brave and just man. All that you have written of late, and the way in which you speak of the "*unnecessary* suffering" of the great mass of humanity, tell me you feel with the people....

She noted that she and her husband, Edward Aveling, "lectured in the States in 1886 on Socialism, and my father's name I am sure you know—Karl Marx." The letter was signed "Eleanor Marx-Aveling."* While in the United States, she and her husband had issued a statement to the press headed "Chicago, 1886" and declaring:

> Eight of the men arrested without warrant were tried by a jury more than one of which had declared their minds to be made up as to the guilt of the accused; before a judge whose every word and deed during the trial was that of an advocate for the prosecution; at a time when most of the American newspapers were clamoring for the blood of these men, upon evidence insufficient to convict a man of picking pockets.

In a speech, she had said, "If the sentence is carried out, it will be one of the most infamous legal murders that have ever been perpetrated.... I am not an Anarchist, but I feel all the more that I am bound to say this."[2]

*For the full text and a facsimile of the letter, see Appendix A.

William Dean Howells was born on March 1, 1837, in Martins Ferry, Ohio, one of the eight children of Mary Dean Howells and William Cooper Howells. Both his father and his paternal grandfather were abolitionists.* At the age of nine he became an apprentice typesetter in his father's printshop. His formal education stopped short of high school, as was common then. During his apprenticeship he read widely, and he was stirred by the writings of William Shakespeare, Miguel de Cervantes, Alexander Pope, and Heinrich Heine. In 1856, he became a reporter for the *Ohio State Journal*, assigned to the capital, Columbus. In 1860, some of his poems appeared in the *Atlantic Monthly*, of which he would later be editor.

So impressive was his campaign biography of Abraham Lincoln, written in 1860, that a year later he was appointed American consul in Venice. Simple, factual, and moving, it had none of the specious political rhetoric so dear to that epoch—and ours. (A facsimile, reproducing Lincoln's handwritten annotations, was published on its centenary.)

Howells married Elinor Mead in 1862, in Paris. She was from an upper-class family in Brattleboro, Vermont, and was a cousin of President Rutherford B. Hayes. They had three children—Winifred, John Mead, and Mildred—and were married for forty-eight years, until her death in 1910.

Howells became assistant editor of the *Atlantic Monthly* in 1865, and from 1871 to 1881 he was its editor. For *Harper's Monthly* he wrote "The Editor's Study" from 1886 to 1892 and "The Editor's Easy Chair" from 1900 until his death in 1920; in 1900 he also began a column in the *North American*

*"Sympathy for the slave had been cardinal in Howells's childhood morality. For that his family had been hounded out of Hamilton, had suffered and failed in Dayton, had fought triumphantly in Ashtabula County," Edwin H. Cady writes, in *The Realist at War*.[3]

Review. In these and other periodicals, he was an unswerving advocate of literary realism and social reform.

Howells helped many young authors, among them Frank Norris, Stephen Crane, Sarah Orne Jewett, Hamlin Garland, Edith Wharton, Booth Tarkington, Mary Wilkins Freeman, and the black writers Paul Laurence Dunbar* and Charles W. Chesnutt. He encouraged Abraham Cahan (who translated part of *A Traveler from Altruria* for his Yiddish Socialist paper) to write *Yekl: A Tale of the New York Ghetto*; found it a publisher; and reviewed it enthusiastically, with Crane's *George's Mother* and *Maggie: A Girl of the Streets* (for whose British edition he wrote a preface). Thorstein Veblen's *The Theory of the Leisure Class* became well known after Howells praised it. He admired the work of his friends Mark Twain and Henry James, and his essays helped introduce American readers to Thomas Hardy, George Moore, George Bernard Shaw, Émile Zola, Henrik Ibsen, Leo Tolstoy, Ivan Turgenev, Fyodor Dostoevsky, and others. Howells's own books—more than one hundred—include novels, stories, literary criticism, travel sketches, plays, memoirs, and poetry.

The poet Edwin Markham, author of "The Man with the Hoe," said, "All men who are patriotic and intelligent should love William Dean Howells as one of the highest and noblest men in the modern world."[4] Harry Thurston Peck, Columbia University professor and editor of the *Bookman*, wrote: "He drank in the subtlest understanding of that stratum of society which is the basis of the whole gigantic system. And for his purpose it was lucky that he never had the academic training which, though it sharpens the critical powers, too often narrows the sympathies and deadens the creative faculty."[5]

*See pages 137–138.

What has inaccurately been called the Haymarket "riot" took place at the corner of Des Plaines and Randolph streets in Chicago on the evening of May 4, 1886, at a meeting to protest the shooting-down of strikers the previous day at the McCormick Harvesting Machine Company. Such gatherings, part of the surging movement for the eight-hour day, invariably ended in brutality by company thugs and the police.

Among those present at Haymarket Square was Mayor Carter Harrison, Sr. He stayed until ten, when the meeting was nearly over and the crowd had dwindled to less than one thousand. Governor John Peter Altgeld wrote later:

> Had the police remained away for twenty minutes more, there would have been nobody left there, but as soon as Captain Bonfield learned that the mayor was gone, he could not resist the temptation to have some more people clubbed, and went up with a detachment of police to disperse the meeting; and on the appearance of the police a bomb was thrown by some unknown person, and several officers, who were simply obeying an uncalled-for order of their superior, were killed.[6]

Seven policemen died; sixty were wounded. Half of these deaths and injuries resulted from wild shooting by the police after the explosion. The exact number of civilian casualties is unknown, since many victims were afraid to go to hospitals. At least four people, perhaps as many as eight, were killed by police gunfire. Approximately fifty were shot or clubbed.

The police jailed and terrorized hundreds of people. Among them were August Spies, Adolph Fischer, Samuel Fielden, George Engel, Michael Schwab, Oscar Neebe, and

Louis Lingg. Above all, they wanted to lay their hands on Albert Parsons, editor of the *Alarm.*

All of the accused, according to Gustavus Myers, were "more or less deep students of economics and sociology; they had become convinced that the fundamental cause of the prevalent inequalities of opportunity and of the widespread misery was the capitalist system itself. Hence they opposed it uncompromisingly."[7] They were all active members of the International Working People's Association.

A manhunt was launched for Parsons, who was hidden by friends in Geneva, Illinois, and Waukesha, Wisconsin. On the eve of the trial he surrendered. Lizzie Holmes, an organizer of Chicago working women, wrote to Caro Lloyd, sister of the reformer and journalist Henry Demarest Lloyd:

> I remember that Mr. Parsons returned to the courthouse in Chicago on the morning of June 21, 1886. He had been safely hidden by my husband, W. T. Holmes, and by Mr. Daniel Hoan* of Waukesha, the only persons in the world who knew where he was.

Mrs. Holmes quoted her husband as saying:

> When I heard he [Parsons] had gone to Chicago to stand trial, I hastened to . . . the jail. I said to him, "Do you know what you have done?" and he said, "Yes, thoroughly. I never expect. . . to be a free man again. They will kill me, but I could not bear to be at liberty knowing that my comrades were here and were to suffer for a crime of which they were as innocent as I."[8]

*His son, Dan Hoan, Jr., later served as Socialist mayor of Milwaukee, 1916–1940.

The defense committee, formed on May 22 and led by Dr. Ernst Schmidt, a respected physician and a Socialist, had hired William R. Black, a corporation lawyer who was deeply sympathetic to the labor movement (though from a Confederate Kentucky family, he had won the Congressional Medal of Honor and attained the rank of captain fighting for the Union in the Civil War); Moses Salomon and Sigmund Zeisler, young lawyers for the Chicago Central Labor Union who had been handling the case since the arrests; and William A. Foster, a criminal lawyer. (Leonard Swett, once Lincoln's law partner, replaced Foster when the verdict was appealed to the Illinois Supreme Court in March 1887.)

Indicted for the murder of Mathias Degan, a policeman, the defendants faced trial on June 21, 1886, before Judge Joseph E. Gary.* They were not charged with throwing the bomb but were tried on the novel legal theory of "constructive crime"—their writings and speeches had allegedly incited some person or persons unknown to commit the outrage.

Judge Gary named a special bailiff to summon a jury of his own selection. There were only five workers in a panel of one thousand, and they were all "excused" by Julius S. Grinnell, the prosecutor. "In vain did the defense try to show that four of the eight accused were not even at the meeting. The men were tried for their political views."[9]

Robert Morss Lovett wrote that some of the accused had spoken at the University of Chicago, where he was a professor of English. At the trial, "a shocking travesty of justice," the judge, "sitting on the bench with prominent ladies beside him as guests, boasted of making the law as he went along."[10]

*A number of writers on Haymarket have confused Joseph E. Gary with Elbert H. Gary, who for many years was chairman of the board of the United States Steel Corporation.

August Spies hurled this challenge at the judge and jury:

> Now, these are my ideas. I cannot divest myself of them, nor would I, if I could. And if you think you can crush out these ideas that are gaining ground more and more every day...by sending us to the gallows, if you would once more have people suffer the penalty of death because they have dared to tell the truth...I say if death is the penalty for proclaiming the truth, then I will proudly and defiantly pay the costly price! Call your hangman! Truth crucified in Socrates, in Christ, in Giordano Bruno, in Hus, in Galileo, still lives. They and others whose name is legion have preceded us in this path. We are ready to follow.[11]

The case went to the jury on August 19, 1886, and the next day all of the accused were declared guilty. Seven were sentenced to be hanged. Neebe received a fifteen-year prison term. This was not entirely unexpected, because the prosecutor had acknowledged that there was no case against him. The role of the press in spreading hysteria and propaganda had been a powerful factor in assuring the convictions.

Anticipating that the Illinois Supreme Court would turn down the appeal, Captain Black and the defense committee engaged three prominent lawyers to carry the fight to the U.S. Supreme Court—Benjamin F. Butler, Union general, governor of Massachusetts, and congressman; John Randolph Tucker, Confederate attorney general of Virginia, congressman, and professor of constitutional law and dean of the law school at Washington and Lee University; and Roger A. Pryor, former journalist and Confederate brigadier-general.

He said, "Outside of my professional capacity as attorney for the men, I fully believe that they were innocent of the crime charged. If there was a plot in existence, do you suppose that they would have had their wives and children there?"[12]

On September 14, 1887, six months after the appeal had been filed, the Illinois Supreme Court denied the writ of error, thus sustaining the convictions. The defendants' lawyers had cited violations of the due-process clause of the Fourteenth Amendment of the Constitution, and of the Fifth and Sixth Amendments, principally in the selection of the jury. An appeal to the United States Circuit Court for a writ of habeas corpus was denied as well, and the judgment was affirmed by the United States Supreme Court on November 2. The executions were to take place on November 11.

On September 25, Howells had written Pryor: "I am glad that you have taken the case of the Chicago Anarchists and that you see some hope for them before the Supreme Court. I have never believed them guilty of murder, or of anything but their opinions. I do not think they were justly convicted.... I venture to... wish you all success in your efforts to save these men."

Two days later, Pryor replied: "It is in harmony with the spirit of justice and humanity of your writings that you desire a fair and legal trial even for Anarchists. Such trial, I assure you on my honor, they have not had, and such trial it is the object of my endeavors to assure them." On October 3, he said: "There is a grave doubt whether, in the whirlwind of passion which swept over Chicago, that the Anarchists have had a fair trial.... A temperate claim on behalf of the Anarchists...under the *imprimatur* of your name cannot but be of wholesome and happy effect."[13]

Howells had already decided to write a letter such as Pryor proposed, but his was to be the only signature. He had asked the abolitionist poet John Greenleaf Whittier, and George W. Curtis, editor of *Harper's Weekly*, to join him. Whittier replied on September 21: "I am opposed to capital punishment and have striven to have the death penalty abolished, but I have never interfered with the law as it affects individual cases. And I can see no reason for making the case of the Anarchists an exception." He ended the letter amiably, "I'm always thy admirer and friend."[14] Howells wrote again on November 1, saying: "A letter from you would have great weight with him [the governor of Illinois, Richard J. Oglesby]. I beseech you to write it and do what one great and blameless man may do to avert the greatest wrong that ever threatened our fame as a nation."[15] It is highly damaging to Whittier's reputation that he later appeared to agree with another poet, James Russell Lowell,* that "the rascals were well hanged."[16]

Howells had written Curtis on August 10: "I feel more than ever that it was not a fair trial either as to the selection of the jury or the rulings of the judge.... They are condemned to death upon a principle that would have sent every ardent anti-slavery man to the gallows." Though he was under great emotional stress because of the baffling malady of his daughter Winifred,† who was being treated at a nearby sanitorium, he was impelled to write again to Curtis, from Lake George, New York, on August 18:

*Lowell had denounced the Mexican War and American slavery in *The Biglow Papers* (1849).

†Her anorexia and other symptoms were diagnosed, in the nebulous medical terminology of the time, as "neurasthenia." She died in March 1889, aged twenty-five, at the Philadelphia sanitorium of Dr. S. Weir Mitchell, an eminent specialist in psychological disorders.

> Of course I feel the force of what you say, and that a man strange to the rules of law should have the ground sure under his feet before he questions the decisions of two courts of law. In my own case you are mistaken as to a "mastery" of the facts. . . . I have had my original feeling that the trial of the Anarchists was hysterical and unjust strengthened by reading a condensed history of it. . . . I feel that these men are doomed to suffer for their opinions' sake. . . . I have spoken with several lawyers . . . and their belief was that the trial was for Socialism and not for murder. I need not say anything to arouse your sympathy in behalf of men who seem to have been persecuted rather than prosecuted, and I will spare you any superfluous rhetoric. But I will own that this case has taken a deep hold of me, and that I feel most strongly the calamity which error in it must embody.[17]

Harper's Weekly claimed on October 1 that the Illinois Supreme Court's denial of the appeal was "universally approved." On November 19, an account of the hangings, illustrated by drawings of Spies in his cell and of death row, and presumably written by Curtis, asserted, "Law and order must be maintained when revolution threatens."[18]

Unquestionably, it was Howells's eminence that led the *New York Tribune* to print his appeal on November 6, 1887:

> As I have petitioned the Governor of Illinois to commute the death penalty of the Anarchists to imprisonment and have also personally written him in their behalf, I ask your leave to express

> here the hope that those who are inclined to do either will not lose faith in themselves because the Supreme Court has denied the condemned a writ of error. That court simply affirmed the legality of the forms under which the Chicago court proceeded; it did not affirm the propriety of trying for murder men fairly indictable for conspiracy alone, and it by no means approved the principle of punishing them because of their frantic opinions, for a crime which they were not shown to have committed. The justice or injustice of their sentence was not before the highest tribunal of our law, and unhappily could not be got there. That question must remain for history, which judges the judgment of courts, to deal with, and I, for one, cannot doubt what the judgment of history will be.
>
> But the worst still is for a very few days reparable; the men sentenced to death are still alive and their lives may be finally saved through the clemency of the Governor, whose prerogative is now this supreme law in their case. I conjure all those who believe that it would be either injustice or impolicy to put them to death to join in urging him by petition, by letter, or through the press, and from the pulpit and the platform, to use his power, in the only direction where it can never be misused, for the mitigation of their punishment.[19]

Henry David, in *The History of the Haymarket Affair*, has noted that not all liberals were equally courageous: "Many gave way before the pressure of the press and the hysteria of fear.... Their property sense dulled their social conscience, and they slipped behind the comforting wall of legality which the courts had erected." Haymarket "brought about the first major 'red scare,' which has rarely been equalled."[20] (David was writing after the Palmer raids of the nineteen-twenties but before the McCarthyite cold-war terror of the nineteen-fifties, with its Smith Act prosecutions, witch-hunts, and blacklists.)

Howells's decision to appeal to the governor of Illinois has been described by George J. Becker as "a revolution in American literature":

> William Dean Howells, who had succeeded Lowell as editor of the *Atlantic Monthly,* who had been offered the succession to the Harvard chair occupied by the exalted figures of Ticknor, Longfellow, and Lowell, and who was already settling into the dignity of dean of American letters which he was to hold for the next thirty years—William Dean Howells, archpriest of the genteel tradition, deserted the study for the arena and published an open letter defending the Chicago anarchists.[21]

"A file of newspaper and magazine clippings in the Howells Papers at Harvard University," Kenneth S. Lynn has commented, "gives a fair indication of the coast-to-coast abuse the novelist sustained as a result of his lonely act of courage."[22] Acutely aware of the risks he was taking, he jeopardized not only his reputation but his livelihood as well.* His wife, Elinor, fully supported his stand.

*Howells was under contract to the conservative firm of Harper and Brothers at a salary of thirteen thousand dollars a year, a fabulous sum in those days. In addition, he was one of America's most popular novelists.

But he did not remain entirely alone. He was soon joined by others, among them Robert Ingersoll, noted lawyer and exponent of agnosticism; Henry Demarest Lloyd; General Matthew M. Trumbull, a veteran of the Mexican War and the Civil War; John Brown, Jr., one of the sons of the great anti-slavery fighter; the radical journalist John Swinton;* and Joseph R. Buchanan, editor of the *Denver Labor Enquirer*. "Ingersoll publicly declared that 'the men were tried during a period of great excitement,' when a fair trial was an impossibility. He said that the court's rulings were wrong. Under the instructions given to the jury by Judge Gary, any man who spoke in favor of a change of government would have been convicted of murder," Henry David writes.[23]

In England the campaign was led by the Socialist artist and writer William Morris. On November 7, he appealed to the poet Robert Browning: "I venture to write you and ask you to sign the enclosed appeal for mercy and so to do what you can to save the lives of seven men who had been condemned to death for a deed of which they were not guilty, after a mere mockery of a trial." On the same day, he told the artist Ford Madox Brown: "In plain words, what they are really to be hanged for is the crime of leading the strikers in their attempt to get the hours of labour shortened. I confess my grief and anger are so great at this miserable murder, and the dastardly way the subject has been treated by the press, that I am not so coherent on the subject as I ought to be."[24] Brown signed the petition, but Browning did not. George Bernard Shaw, who joined Morris, Peter Kropotkin, and others at a mass rally in London, made the scathing remark, "If seven men must die for the Haymarket explosion,

*See "John Swinton, Crusading Editor," in this volume.

civilization can better afford to lose the seven members of the Illinois Supreme Court." Kropotkin called the case "a retaliation upon prisoners taken in the virtual civil war that is going on between the two classes."[25]

Art Young, who would become a noted radical artist, later recalled: "From England, protests against the executions were cabled by William Morris, Walter Crane, Annie Besant, and Oscar Wilde. On a single day, sixteen thousand members of working-class organizations in London signed a plea to Governor Oglesby. George Bernard Shaw was one of those who circulated the petition."[26] In *William Morris, Romantic to Revolutionary*, E. P. Thompson writes:

> Bismarck's anti-Socialist law had attracted favorable attention in England, and the judicial murder of the anarchists in Chicago...had emboldened reactionaries to preach openly from the text "Go thou, and do likewise." On the day after the Chicago executions...the *Times* [of London] published a remarkable editorial, denouncing the public petitions throughout the United States for clemency to the anarchists as "a mischievous practice and an unparalleled amount of illegitimate pressure," and complaining at the lax discipline which enabled Lingg...to disappoint the hangman."*[27]

The left wing of France's Chamber of Deputies petitioned Governor Oglesby to commute the death sentences.

At their friends' urging, Spies, Schwab, and Fielden wrote the governor one week before they were to be hanged:

*See page 122.

> In order that the truth may be known by you, and the public you represent, we desire to state that we never advocated the use of force, except in cases of self-defense. To accuse us of having attempted to overthrow law and government on May 4, 1886, or at any other time, is as false as it is absurd. Whatever we said or did was said and done publicly; we have never conspired or plotted to commit an unlawful act. While we attacked the present social arrangements in writing and speech, and exposed their iniquities, we have never consciously broken any laws. So far from having planned the killing of anybody at the Haymarket, the very object of the meeting was to protest against the commission of murder. All our efforts have been in the direction to elevate mankind, and to remove as much as possible the cause of crime in society. Our labor was unselfish; no notion of personal gain or ambition prompted us. Thousands and thousands will bear testimony to this. We may have erred at times in our judgment—yes, we may have "loved mankind not wisely, but too well."*[28]

The press had been venomous even before Haymarket. At a mass meeting on July 22, 1877, supporting the nationwide rail strike, Albert Parsons had denounced the press, and the *Chicago Tribune* in particular. He said that an eight-hour day was the only way to avoid the unemployment caused by machinery meant to "rationalize" the labor force. Next morning the *Tribune* counterattacked, demanding that railwaymen

*For a facsimile of the letter, see Appendix B.

who refused to take wage cuts and dismissal notices "step out of the way.... If they will not step out voluntarily, they must be made to by force." The strikers were "the scum and filth of the city." The *Tribune* asserted three days later, "Capitalism would offer any sum to see the leaders...strung up to a telegraph pole."[29] Yet, only a year earlier, on America's centennial, July 4, 1876, the *Tribune* had loftily observed, "Suddenly acquired wealth, decked in all the colors of the rainbow, flaunts its robes before the eyes of labor, and laughs with contempt at honest poverty."[30] Two years prior to Haymarket, the *Tribune* had declared: "The simplest plan, probably, when one is not a member of the Humane Society, is to put arsenic in the supplies of food furnished the unemployed or the tramp. This produces death in a short time and is a warning to other tramps to keep out of the neighborhood."[31]

The Haymarket issue provided Theodore Roosevelt with an opportunity to display his brand of "Americanism." A candidate for mayor of New York City against Henry George in 1886, Roosevelt was flexing his muscles at his ranch in the Dakota Territory. Asked for his stand on the case, he wrote: "My men [presumably the workers on his ranch] are hard-working laboring men who work longer hours for no greater wages than most of the strikers; but they are *Americans through and through.* I believe nothing would give them greater pleasure than a chance with rifles at one of the mobs." In an 1888 article, this much-publicized big-game hunter and imperialist declared, "The day that the Anarchists were hung in Chicago, my men joined with the rest of the neighborhood in burning them in effigy.[32]

In 1887, the steel magnate Andrew Carnegie proclaimed, "I defy any man to show that there is pauperism in the United States."[33] At that moment, millions were suffering from unemployment and privation. Terence V. Powderly, head of the increasingly conservative Knights of Labor, chided, "At Chicago the sound of the bomb did more injury to the good name of labor than all the attacks of that year."[34] But Nathan Fine writes, in *Labor and Farmer Parties in the United States*: "Contrary to the oft-expressed easy generalization that the Haymarket bomb destroyed the Chicago labor movement, the fact is that despite police repression, newspaper incitement to hysteria, and organization of the possessing classes, which followed the throwing of the bomb on May 4, 1886, the Chicago wage-earners only united their forces and stiffened their resistance."[35]

Alone of New York's English-language press, which then included many newspapers, *John Swinton's Paper* retained some measure of sanity. Swinton wrote on August 22, 1886, that it was impossible to comprehend how any jury could have convicted the defendants "upon the flimsy and perjured evidence of the spies and informers who were the principal witnesses against them."[36]

Howells was by no means the only individual who, in the shock of Haymarket, perceived the inadequacy and injustice of the social order. Eighteen-year-old Emma Goldman, who had come to the United States in 1886, was horrified by the trial and the executions. Years later, when she was a noted Anarchist and feminist, she recalled: "The next morning I woke as from a long illness. I had a distinct sensation that something new and wonderful had been born in my soul—a great ideal, a burning faith, a determination to dedicate myself to the memory of my martyred comrades, to make their cause my own, to make known to the world their beautiful lives and heroic deaths."[37]

In October 1887 a mass meeting was held in the Great Hall of Cooper Union, in New York City. Among the speakers were Samuel Gompers, president of the American Federation of Labor; Peter McGuire, founder of the United Brotherhood of Carpenters and Joiners, and, with Gompers, of the AFL; and Daniel De Leon, a young lecturer on international law at Columbia University. He said, "I come here deliberately and for the good name of our beloved country, that its proud record shall not be bloodstained by a judicial crime such as the one contemplated in Chicago."[38] By 1890 De Leon had joined the Socialist Labor Party, later becoming its leader. In 1905 he helped found the Industrial Workers of the World.

But Art Young was deceived by the propaganda, even after he sketched the prisoners for the *Chicago Daily News* (he was not, however, permitted to talk with them):

> Not until several years later did I discover that there was another side to the story. So when asked by a publisher to draw a cover for a paper-bound anti-Anarchist book, I readily assented. *Anarchists and Bomb-Throwers* was the title of this volume, and it upheld the convictions. My picture showed Law and Order, personified by an Amazonian woman, throttling a bunch of dangerous-looking men. If the dead can hear, I ask forgiveness now for that act. I was young and I had been misled by the clamor of many voices raised to justify a dark and shameful deed.[39]

Perhaps the most dramatic record of Howells's reaction to the case, according to Professor Howard A. Wilson of Knox College, is a series of letters to William Mackintire Salter, a Unitarian minister who was the lecturer of the Chicago

Society for Ethical Culture.[40] Salter's view of the case was contradictory, and he soon changed it, as he became deeply involved in the clemency movement. Though he opposed the death sentences, he believed at first that Engel, Fischer, and Lingg had been accessories to murder, inciting violence by their words, whereas the evidence again Parsons, Spies, Fielden, Schwab, and Neebe "is not such as to convince any fair-minded, unprejudiced man beyond reasonable doubt." But he added: "I do not say that because the four I have mentioned are not guilty, they are therefore guiltless of any connection whatever with the Haymarket crime. They are simply not guilty of the *crime with which they were charged.* They were not accessories to the murder of Degan. . . . They were guilty of sedition, of stirring up insurrection. They were all guilty of a conspiracy against the State."[41]

Howells wrote Salter on November 1, 1887:

> I have read with grateful satisfaction your discourse on the condemned Anarchists. I have never thought they had a fair trial, and I find by your statement of the case that I had clearly acquainted myself with the facts. I have already both signed a petition for commutation of their sentences and written a letter to the governor on their behalf. Is there any hope of his clemency? Is there anything more to be done? Take a moment to write me a line. I feel deeply in this matter. You may remember meeting me at Prof. James's in Cambridge. If you do, kindly present my regards to Mrs. Salter.*[42]

*Mary, Salter's wife, and Alice, wife of the Harvard philosopher William James (brother of Henry James), were sisters.

On November 3, Mrs. Salter thanked Howells for his clemency appeal:

> It will doubtless influence many. My husband has sent copies of his petition to the East—Boston, Cambridge, and New York—and is devoting all of his time and strength to circulating it here. Popular opinion is in favor of the carrying out of the sentence, the press having been particularly bloodthirsty, but men of great weight in the city—a few—are beginning to be heard advocating mercy, and Mr. Salter feels that if there were a little more time, much might be accomplished in the way of getting it.[43]

On the same day, Spies wrote:

> My dear Mr. Salter:
>
> Captain Black has written an appeal to the governor signed by some of us which contains essentially the same statements. Whether under the circumstances it is wise to present the letter I enclose in this also—this you may decide. I think it would be well if you would simply explain to the governor orally any things that he does not seem to understand. I am, as a matter of course, sorry for the poor devils who lost their lives at the Haymarket, but I am more so for the lives of the poor devils who perished on the previous day. Who cares for their wretched families? Nobody. Now, for me to express condolences over the killing of the policemen, and not at the same time over that of the poor fellows at McCormick's or

> at East St. Louis,* would be an act of hypocrisy such as I would not be guilty of under any circumstances. Suffice it to say that I abhor murder in *every* form. If I did not I would never have become a Socialist!
>
> Whether or not to make use of the accompanying letter, I leave entirely to your good judgment.
>
> Thanking you for the keen interest you have taken in our case, I am
>
> Yours very truly,
> A. Spies†[44]

Spies had been acquainted with Salter prior to Haymarket. On March 18, 1884, he had invited Salter to speak at the Chicago Turnverein (one of the many societies of foreign-born workers) "on behalf of betterment of our public schools.... As you undoubtedly know, the Common Council of this city, under the inspiration of the Roman Church, opposes the establishment of a more perfect school system than the present one by withholding the necessary funds."[45]

In 1951, Professor John W. Ward of the University of Minnesota called attention to "an unnoticed and uncollected Howells letter on Haymarket. This deserves to be rescued from obscurity." It too was written on November 3, to the poet Francis Fisher Browne, editor of the *Dial*:

> Thank you for sending me your poem, which I read with a heavy heart because of that "impending tragedy." For many weeks, for months, it has not been for one hour out of my waking thoughts;

*In 1886, deputized gunmen and the police killed striking McCormick workers in Chicago and railway switchmen in East St. Louis.

†For a facsimile of the letter, see Appendix C.

> it is the last thing when I lie down, and the first thing when I rise up. It blackens my life. I feel the horror and the shame of the crime which the law is about to commit against justice.[46]

Browne showed the letter to Henry Demarest Lloyd on November 7. Though Howells had not intended it to be made public, they felt that it might prove helpful to the condemned men. On November 8, 1887, the *Chicago Tribune* published Howells's letter, with the headline "Mr. Howells Is Distressed," below one by the meat-packing magnate Philip Armour, just back from a tour of the West with the report that "the entire nation" supported the verdict. This was "no time for maudlin sentiment or foolish tears," Armour admonished. On November 11 Howells wrote Browne:

> It is all right. My pride suffered some twinges when I saw my letter in the *Tribune* with the insulting headline the night editor had given it, for I perceived that what was written for the eye of a friend was somewhat hysterical in print. But if you and other humane persons believed that it might do good—even so little where so much was needed—you did right, and I approved and adopt your action. I don't know yet what the governor has done. While I write, that hideous scene may be enacting in your jail yard—the thing forever damnable before God and abominable to civilized men. But while I don't know, I can still hope.[47]

On November 9, he had wired Salter, "Please telegraph me the governor's decision about the Anarchists."*[48] At

*For a facsimile of Salter's November 11 telegram, see Appendix D.

seven that evening, Governor Oglesby issued a statement saying that he had commuted to life imprisonment the sentences of Schwab and Fielden. But he refused to act on the clemency appeals of Spies, Fischer, and Engel. (Parsons had not made an appeal.) Early on the morning of November 10, the police reported that Lingg had died after exploding a dynamite cap in his mouth.* Shortly after twelve noon on November 11, Parsons, Spies, Fischer, and Engel were hanged.

The next day, in a long letter that he wrote to *New York Tribune* but probably did not send, Howells said:

> I have borne with what patience I must, during the past fortnight, to be called by the *Tribune*, day after day, imbecile and bad citizen, with the others who desired mercy for the men killed yesterday at Chicago, in conformity with our still barbarous laws.... We have committed an atrocious and irreparable wrong.... Their trial has not been a trial by justice, but a trial by passion, by terror, by prejudice, by hate, by newspaper.[49]

To his father Howells wrote on November 13:

> I send you the [November 6 *New York*] *Tribune*, with my unavailing word for the Anarchists. All is over now, except the judgment that begins at once for every unjust and evil deed and goes on forever. The historical perspective is that this free Republic has killed five men for their opinions....I have had many letters thanking me for my words.... Of course I get abuse in print, but that doesn't matter.[50]

*For contrary views, see Appendix E, page 163.

One letter, from the novelist Harriet Prescott Spofford, said, "Great as your work is, you never wrote more immortal words than those in behalf of the men who are dying for free speech." Elinor Howells's cousin Edwin D. Mead, editor of the *New England* magazine, and later director of the World Peace Foundation, was also sympathetic. Howells wrote him on November 13:

> I got your postal while I still had some foolish hope that the lives of these helpless men could be saved. Of course I never doubted where you stood—it was as if I touched your true hand in the dark and knew that you were beside the few not drunk and blind with the fear and hate that seem to have debauched this nation. . . . I too had studied the case, and found none of the men connected by credible proof with any "plot" against society's forces on the occasion of the policeman's murder, for which they were convicted.[51]

Howells asked Salter on November 14: "Do send me a copy of your review of the Anarchist case. I sent mine to a great and good man whom I was fool enough to hope I might move to join in the plea for mercy."[52] He had told Whittier on November 1, 'I enclose a paper on the Anarchists by a very good and a very able young minister of Chicago."

The cataclysmic destruction of his illusions continued to oppress him. He told his sister Annie Howells Fréchette on November 18:

> Elinor and I both no longer care for the world's life and would like to be settled down very humbly and simply, where we could be socially identified with the principles of progress and sympathy for

> the struggling mass.... The last two months have been full of heartache and horror for me, on account of the civic murder committed last Friday at Chicago. You may have seen in the papers that I had taken part in petitioning for clemency for the Anarchists, whom I thought unfairly tried, and most unjustly condemned. Annie, it's all been an atrocious piece of frenzy and cruelty, for which we must stand ashamed forever before history. But it's no use. I can't write about it. Someday I hope to do justice to these irreparably wronged men.[53]

On November 20, Howells wrote Salter:

> I'm greatly in your debt for all those papers, which I read with the helpless grief and rage which seem to be my part of this business. But now that the worst has happened, can't we do something to begin the work of history concerning those men? I have suggested to Mr. Browne of the *Dial* the publication of a book embodying expressions of sympathy and protest from those who made them, and a narrative of the efforts of the clemency committees.... What do you think of the plan? The profits of the book should go to the dead men's families.[54]

He wrote Salter again on November 24:

> I shall be glad to get poor Spies's letter, which it wrung my heart to read in print. Do you mean to give it to me? By the way, I should like to have fotografs of the four murdered men, in fact of the

whole eight accused.... Did you see that letter I printed in the *New York Tribune*, Nov. 6? All the papers abused it, but few copied it. What a squalid and vulgar oligarchy of half-bred scribblers we live under! Somehow their power must be broken.... It still seems impossible those four men should have been killed two weeks ago. Think of Parsons actually coming back, from safety, and giving himself up to that incredible death! Was ever a generous man so atrociously dealt with before? I don't understand how you could get through it all, unbroken.[55]

On December 1, he wrote Salter:

I don't know how to thank you enough for the gift of poor Spies's note. I value it most highly; it seems to be the touch of a dying man on my hand. I suppose that you and I both have the same reservations in regard to him, but we must both allow that he was a noble, unselfish, and heroic soul. We ought not to leave his memory and that of the others to infamy; but I can well understand why Mr. Browne cannot undertake the memorial. I cannot because my Harper engagement covers all my work; but can't you? I will contribute a letter—the only form not cut off by my contract—and I will help you in any way I can. Wouldn't Mr. Lloyd associate himself with you in the work? I read and will read again Mr. Lloyd's address to the governor. How could that man resist such facts? In New York I met Mr. O. J. Smith of the American Press Association,

> who said he knew the bailiff who "fixed" the jury: a perfectly unmoral creature. General Pryor, with whom I had been in correspondence since he took up the Anarchists' case, asked me to dinner, and there I met half a dozen men of our thinking. He told me that *after* their case was lost with the U.S. Supreme Court, the Anarchists paid him and the others up in full. Spies wrote to thank him the day he was murdered.[56]

Browne's publisher would not permit him to edit the book, and the idea was later abandoned.

A New York lawyer, Courtlandt Palmer, founder of the Nineteenth-Century Club, had taken part in the clemency campaign and spoke at a Cooper Union memorial meeting on November 28. Howells wrote him on December 7:

> I send you my only copy of the [November 6 *New York*] *Tribune* letter, but yours much more nearly expresses my mind. I did not know you had written anything, but I wished when I read what you said at that meeting to send you a *stretto a mano* [handshake]. What courage and nobleness of heart you showed in writing that letter in the midst of the base terrorism that weighed upon the minds and souls of men in those forever infamous days. The nation remains dishonored till the memory of the victims of civic murder at Chicago is rehabilitated. I am trying to get someone there to put together a record of the clemency movement, and your letter should be in it.[57]

Howells thanked Salter for Spies's picture on December 11, exactly a month after the executions: "I think of these men every day, and of the wrong their names are under, and long to have them righted before the world. The fotograf of Spies is most interesting. What an intelligent, earnest, *good* face! And that man hanged! Incredible!"[58]

On December 25, he wrote Salter: "The press continues as atrocious as ever, but I believe it never fairly represented the whole sentiment of the community. Every now and then I hear of some good man who loathed that injustice as we did.... Do you know about the case of Rev. J. C. Kimball, of Hartford, who preached a clemency sermon and met with persecution in his community? I will send you his pamphlet."[59] John C. Kimball, pastor of the First Unitarian Congregational Society, had compared the hangings to the crucifixion. "A motion to eject him was roundly defeated and a resolution passed that the society was proud to have in its pulpit ministers who 'were in advance of the public sentiment...and dared again and again to take an unpopular side.'"[60]

Howells wrote Hamlin Garland on January 15, 1888:

> You'll easily believe that I did not bring myself to the point of openly befriending these men who were civically murdered for their opinions without thinking and feeling much, and my horizons have been infinitely widened by the process....I am reading and thinking about questions that carry me beyond myself and my miserable little idolatries of the past. Perhaps you'll find that I've been writing about them.[61]

Howells was referring to *Annie Kilburn* (1888), his novel about a New England mill town.

On April 5 he wrote Mark Twain: "If ever a public was betrayed by its press, it's ours. No man could safely make himself heard in behalf of the strikers* any more than for the Anarchists. . . . By the way, have you seen Rev. Kimball yet? When you do, give him my regards."[62] Twain, who lived in Hartford, knew of Kimball's sermon and presumably had read the pamphlets that Howells had sent him in March, but their correspondence gives no indication of his feelings about the case. He had already fallen into the mood of fatalism and pessimism that was to characterize the rest of his life.

To the critic Thomas Sergeant Perry, Howells wrote on April 14: "I enclose my letter about the Anarchists, which I wrote just before their civic murder. I came to that mind about it through reading the trial, in which they proved themselves absolutely guiltless of the murder charged upon them; but it was predetermined to kill them. They died with unsurpassable courage."[63]

The writer and Unitarian minister Edward Everett Hale had praised *Annie Kilburn*, which *Harper's Monthly* was serializing, and Howells replied on August 30:

> The most that I can do is perhaps to set a few people thinking, for as yet I haven't got to *doing* anything, myself. But at present it seems to me that our competitive civilization is a state of warfare and a game of chance, in which each man fights and bets against fearful odds. . . . John will gladly join your [Harvard] Tolstoy Club. He's read a great deal of Tolstoy, and has had him much talked into him.[64]

In the novel, the Reverend Julius Peck rejects the ineffectual and patronizing charity of his wealthy parishioners, preaching instead a gospel of social justice.

*See pages 14 and 15.

To Henry James, Howells wrote on October 10: "I should hardly like to trust pen and ink with all the audacity of my social ideas; but after fifty years of optimistic content with "civilization" and its ability to come out all right in the end, I now abhor it and feel that it is coming out all wrong in the end, unless it bases itself anew on a real equality."[65] (Though James rarely dealt with political themes, his 1886 novel *The Princess Casamassima* depicts a London Anarchist group.)

In a long letter to the *New York Sun* that Howells wrote on November 23 but never sent, he said:

> Since when were courts infallible? I am old enough to remember a decision of even the Supreme Court of the United States (in the case of Dred Scott) which provoked the dissent of a good half, at least, of the American people. I recall with still greater distinctness the discussion of the John Brown case after the court had dealt with it. Was this discussion legitimate, or not?... As soon as any legal decision is rendered, the question of its rightness begins. In this very case of the Anarchists, it began in all the newspapers; and it seems to me that I had the same right to declare it unjust that the newspapers used to declare it just. The laws are made not only for judges to expound, but for every common man like me to understand for himself; or else they are a cruel mockery.... You say I was among the "sentimentalists" who petitioned the governor of Illinois for mercy to the condemned Anarchists. I own with joy that I was of those who did so ask mercy; but I cannot consent to be called a sentimentalist for that reason. Ex-Senator Lyman Trumbull

> of Illinois and the eminent journalist Henry D. Lloyd were of them, too, as well as attorneys like Ingolf Boyesen, and three or four judges of Chicago courts. Do you call such men sentimentalists; if you do, why? Did they ask mercy because they were sentimentalists, or did they become sentimentalists by virtue of that act?[66]

On June 26, 1893, nearly six years after the Haymarket martyrs had stood on the scaffold, and one day after the monument in Waldheim Cemetery was dedicated, Governor John Peter Altgeld freed the three prisoners. His "Reasons for Pardoning Fielden, Neebe, and Schwab" were:

> First, that the jury was a packed jury selected to convict; second, that according to the law as laid down by the Supreme Court, both prior to and again since the trial of this case, the jurors, according to their own answers, were not competent jurors and the trial was therefore not a legal trial; third, that the defendants were not proven guilty of the crime charged in the indictment; fourth, that as to the defendant Neebe, the state's attorney had declared at the close of the evidence that there was no case against him, and yet he has been kept in prison all these years; fifth, that the trial judge was either so prejudiced against the defendants, or else so determined to win the applause of a certain class in the community, that he could not and did not grant a fair trial.... It is further shown that much of the evidence was a pure fabrication; that some prominent police officials, in their zeal, not only terrorized ignorant

> men by throwing them into prison and threatening them with torture if they refused to swear to anything desired but offered money and employment to those who would consent to do this; further, that they deliberately planned to have fictitious conspiracies formed in order that they might get the glory of discovering them.[67]

The first signature on the pardon petition was that of the banker Lyman J. Gage, later Secretary of the Treasury under McKinley and Roosevelt. Among the sixty thousand names were those of Edward S. Dreyer and John N. Hills, who had served on the grand jury that indicted the eight men. But despite the growing conviction that they had been framed, Altgeld's carefully documented forty-page statement created a firestorm of hatred: "Newspapers across the country united in heaping abuse on the man who had 'opened the gates' to anarchy.... What offended most of his critics was that he had called the sanctity of the judicial process into question, and with a body of evidence so overwhelming that it could not be easily refuted," writes Paul Avrich.[68]

Altgeld, the first Democratic governor of Illinois since the Civil War, remained influential in his party and was nominated again in 1896. But he lost the election after a bitter campaign—he was reviled for both the Haymarket pardon and his opposition to the use of federal troops to break the 1894 Pullman strike—though he received fifty thousand more votes than in 1892. He resumed the practice of law, and in 1901 the noted labor lawyer Clarence Darrow invited him to join his firm. They remained colleagues until Altgeld's death the following year.

Darrow recalled that it had not taken long for the Illinois bar to conclude that the verdict had been "brought about through malice and hatred, and that the trial itself was unfair and the judgment of the court unsound."[69] He pointed out that Fielden, Parsons, and Schwab had barely been acquainted with Engel, Fischer, and Lingg. Moreover, Judge Gary had wrongly permitted the prosecution to incorporate into the record of the trial the files of Spies's newspaper, the *Arbeiter-Zeitung* (*Workers' Newspaper*), and Parsons's paper, the *Alarm*, as well as speeches given by Parsons in various cities over many years. Concocting his own rules of evidence, Gary instructed the jurors that if they believed these articles and speeches had led to the throwing of the bomb, they had to find the defendants guilty of murder.

Darrow had often visited Fielden, Neebe, and Schwab in the Illinois State Penitentiary at Joliet. He "had come to love them as good and honest men, guilty only of the crime of striving to free mankind from its shackles."[70] He always regretted not having been one of the lawyers in the case.*

In "The Martyred Apostles of Labor," an article in the *New Time* of February 1898, the noted Socialist and labor leader Eugene V. Debs wrote: "The men who were judicially murdered in Chicago in 1887, in the great state of Illinois, were the advance couriers of a better day. They were called Anarchists, but at their trial it was not proven that they had

*Darrow later defended Eugene V. Debs and the American Railway Union (1894); Charles Moyer, William ("Big Bill") Haywood, and George Pettibone of the Western Federation of Miners (1907); James B. and John J. McNamara in the *Los Angeles Times* bombing case (1911); twenty Communist Labor Party members in Chicago, including Max Bedacht, Charles Krumbein, and William Bross Lloyd, son of Henry Demarest Lloyd (1920); and Dr. Ossian Sweet, a black physician charged with murder for defending his Detroit home against an armed racist mob (1925).

committed any crime or violated any law. They had protested against unjust laws and their brutal administration."[71]

Debs's admiration for one of their staunchest defenders is shown by four items in his scrapbooks: an article from the *Indianapolis News* (November 19, 1899) about Howells's lecture there on "Novels and Novel-Writing," during his six-week Midwestern tour (Debs's home was in Terre Haute); Mark Twain's praise of Howells's literary art (June 1906); Howells's contribution to a symposium on death (March 1910); and this excerpt from his tribute to Twain (September 1910): "The last time I saw him alive was made memorable to me by the kind, clear, judicial sense with which he explained and justified the labor unions as the sole present help of the weak against the strong."[72] To Hamlin Garland, Howells wrote on April 5, 1895, "A good fellow named Darrow, one of Debs's lawyers, was here the other day, and we spoke of you." On April 28, he asked, "Do you know that good fellow Darrow, who helped defend Debs before the Supreme Court? He's important, and solid; most interesting."[73]

On October 7, 1910, Howells recalled the emotions of a quarter-century earlier, in his reply to a letter from the playwright Percy W. MacKaye, who was writing a biography of his father, the actor and playwright J. M. Steele MacKaye:

> I had but one meeting with your father: at the house of Judge Pryor in 1887, where several of us came together in sympathy with him when he was trying—or had vainly tried—to get the U.S. Supreme Court to grant the Chicago Anarchists a new trial. With your father I believed that the men had been condemned on an unjust ruling, and condemned for their opinions and not for a proven crime. I wish I could recall details of

> that most interesting night; but I remember your father's wrathful fervor, and instances he alleged of police brutality. I remember his vivid personality, and the glimpses it gave of a magnanimous manhood.[74]

It would be unjust to believe that Howells's conscience was stirred solely by the Haymarket outrage. Six years earlier—in 1880—he had accepted for publication in the *Atlantic Monthly* "The Story of a Great Monopoly," Henry Demarest Lloyd's exposé of the buccaneering practices of the Standard Oil Company. (This was a precursor of Ida M. Tarbell's later revelations.) The *Atlantic* had printed articles criticizing ruthless, free-enterprise big business, but never one so damning as Lloyd's. Howells played a key role in presenting such an exposé to an important segment of society. Robert L. Hough, in *The Quiet Rebel*, writes:

> The impact on the country of Lloyd's disclosures of secret rebates, extortion, bribery, and perjury was considerable. An unprecedented seven printings of the magazine had to be run off before the demand was satisfied, and Lloyd's article was widely reprinted in newspapers, particularly in the West. It is of course significant that the forerunner of the muckraking articles should appear in a magazine edited by William Dean Howells. To accept such an essay in 1880 took a great deal of courage, for Americans, proud of their progress and material wealth, often looked upon the big corporations and trusts as major contributors to this advancement. Yet Howells apparently took the risk with no misgivings.[75]

In 1894, after four publishers had rejected Lloyd's book *Wealth Against Commonwealth*, Howells persuaded Harper and Brothers to take it. On November 2 he wrote Lloyd:

> To think that the monstrous iniquity whose story you tell so powerfully accomplished itself in our lifetime is so astounding, so infuriating, that I have to stop from chapter to chapter and take breath. So prosperity was destroyed and law baffled and justice bought in lands where freedom never was, but surely not in this land of liberty. The truth is so repulsive that one almost wishes that the Standard might come to one's relief with a lie of the sort which has made it irresistible everywhere but in your pages. I do not know what effect your book will have in this generation, but hereafter it will form the source from which all must draw who try to paint the evilest phase of the century.[76]

Haymarket—like a bolt of lightning—was unquestionably the single searing experience that fused Howells's critique of his society and tore away the last cobwebs of illusion. The lasting effects of the trauma that he underwent are clearly demonstrated in his later development as a novelist and critic. The bibliographical note to his novel *A Hazard of New Fortunes* (1890) is significant: "The shedding of blood, which is for the remission of sins, had been symbolized by the bombs and scaffolds of Chicago.... Opportunely for me, there was a great streetcar strike in New York, and the story began to find its way to issues nobler and larger than those of the love affairs common to fiction."[77]

Some years later, Theodore Dreiser too was stirred by,

and drawn into, the drama of a streetcar strike, which he depicted when he drew the memorable figure of Hurstwood in decline, in *Sister Carrie*. Dreiser, his novels still unwritten, his ordeals with censorship still to be undergone, had found Howells "truly generous and humane, a wholly honest man."[78] While working as a free-lance writer, Dreiser interviewed him in April 1898, for the magazine *Success*. Howells answered a number of questions about his career and then concluded by saying: "I have come to see life, not as the chase of a forever-impossible personal happiness, but as a field for endeavor toward the happiness of the whole human family. There is no other success."[79]

In the same year, Howells said in the *American Fabian*, "It was ten years ago that I first became interested in the creed of Socialism." While his daughter Winifred was in an upstate New York sanitorium, he had attended a lecture in Buffalo by the Danish-born Socialist Laurence Gronlund, and then read and reviewed his book *The Cooperative Commonwealth* (1884).* He also read Henry George's *Progress and Poverty* (1879), essays on Socialism by William Morris, and by George Bernard Shaw and other members of the British Fabian Society, and three utopian novels—W. H. Hudson's *A Crystal Age* (1887), Edward Bellamy's *Looking Backward* (1888), and Morris's *News from Nowhere* (1891). "The greatest influence, however, came to me through reading Tolstoy."[81] Howells was stirred both by Tolstoy's literary work and by the Christian Socialism he espoused. In his 1888 letter to the *New York Sun*, he had said, "When it comes to my 'Socialism,' are you quite sure of your facts . . . beyond my well-known admiration

*Friedrich Engels, in a letter to Friedrich Sorge from London (July 3, 1885), was less than enthusiastic about Gronlund's political theories.[80]

for Tolstoy as a man and an artist, and my respectful attitude towards the books of Laurence Gronlund?"

It was Howells who brought to public notice the young black writer Paul Laurence Dunbar, who was employed as an elevator operator in Dayton, Ohio, at a weekly wage of four dollars. Howells enthusiastically reviewed his second book of poems, *Majors and Minors* (1895), and wrote a preface for his next book, *Lyrics of Lowly Life* (1896): "His brilliant and unique achievement is to have studied the American Negro objectively and to have represented him as he found him to be, with humor, with sympathy, and yet with what the reader must instinctively feel to be entire truthfulness.... He has made the strongest claim for the Negro in English literature that the Negro has yet made."[82]

In a letter that he wrote Howells on July 13, 1896, thanking him for his review, Dunbar said that he felt as though he had "suddenly been knighted" by Howells's acclaim: "I can tell you nothing about myself because there is nothing to tell. My whole life has been simple, obscure, and uneventful."[83] Howells arranged for Dunbar to be represented by a literary agent and a lecture bureau. After giving a series of readings in America and Britain, Dunbar obtained a position at the Library of Congress, with the help of Robert Ingersoll. He died in 1906, aged thirty-three, having written seven books of verse, four collections of short stories, and four novels.

Brand Whitlock, author, reform mayor of Toledo, and U.S. minister to Belgium, described Dunbar's first meeting with Howells, in 1896:

> The pride and delight Dunbar found in the visit were most charming to witness. It was late in September when this occurred, and as he was

> about to leave Mr. Howells noticed that Dunbar had no overcoat. So he insisted, against protest, that Dunbar wear his.... The coat was much too large for Dunbar's slender frame, and he might have wrapped it about himself twice. The next day Dunbar returned the garment with a note of thanks, in which he confessed that he felt honored by wearing the great coat, though he was sure he was "an ass in the lion's skin."[84]

In 1893, Whitlock, as chief clerk to the Illinois secretary of state, William H. Hinrichsen, had prepared the pardons that accompanied Governor Altgeld's statement:

> It mattered not that most of the thoughtful men in Illinois would tell you that the "Anarchists" had been improperly convicted, that they not only were entirely innocent, but were not even Anarchists; it was simply that the mob had convicted them, in one of the strangest frenzies of fear that ever distracted a whole community.... And so, one morning in June, very early, I was called to the governor...and told to make out pardons for Fielden, Neebe, and Schwab.[85]

The black leader Dr. W. E. B. Du Bois paid tribute to Howells in the *Crisis* in 1913. He mentioned Howells's novella about racial prejudice, *An Imperative Duty* (1893); his sponsorship of Dunbar; and the fact that Howells was among the first signers of the document calling for the founding of the National Association for the Advancement of Colored People. After his death, Dr. Du Bois called him "perhaps the most distinguished of American authors."[86]

In Howells's novel *A Traveler from Altruria* (1894), the wealthy Mrs. Makely says, "In spite of our divisions and classes we are all Americans, and if we haven't the same opinions and ideas on minor matters, we all have the same country." But the young worker Reuben Camp responds:

> I don't know about that. I don't believe we all have the same country. America is one thing for you, and it's quite another thing for us. America means ease, and comfort, and amusement for you, year in and year out, and if it means work, it's work that you *wish* to do. For us, America means work that we *have* to do, and hard work, all the time, if we're going to make both ends meet. It means liberty for you; but what liberty has a man got who doesn't know where his next meal is coming from? Once I was on strike, when I was working on the railroad, and I've seen men come and give up their liberty for a chance to earn their family's living. They knew they were right, and that they ought to have stood up for their rights, but they had lie down and lick the hand that fed them. Yes, we are all Americans, but I guess we haven't all got the same country, Mrs. Makely. What sort of country has a blacklisted man got?[87]

About another novel of this period, Daniel Aaron writes, "One of his most trenchant critiques of plutocratic values, *A Hazard of New Fortunes* links the Civil War directly with the class conflicts of the post–Civil War Gilded Age, chattel slavery with wage slavery."[88] *The Quality of Mercy* (1892) and *The World of Chance* (1893) also focus on social injustice.

In the Marxist literary journal *Mainstream*, Charles Olson comments, "If Howells's utopian Socialism prevented him from seeing what, in the final analysis, had to be done, he knew nevertheless that capitalism was America's cancer, and that only the most fundamental changes could cure it."[89]

He advocated "nationalization of natural monopolies—railroads, express and telegraph lines, gas and water works, and telephone and electric-power circuits; preservation of the public domain and establishment of national parks; government aid and subsidies to farmers; public employment for the relief of the jobless; public control of housing; government-subsidized theater; old-age pensions; and state-managed inns along public roads."[90] Like Gronlund and Bellamy, Howells believed that it was the responsibility of "the intellectual classes" to lead the way to Socialism. The three men shared the notion that the capitalists could somehow be persuaded that their best interests, too, would thus be served.

But Howells was not entirely convinced of this, as a letter to Mark Twain suggests. Twain was pleased that the Brazilian monarchy had been overthrown just one month before his novel *A Connecticut Yankee in King Arthur's Court* was published, but he complained that the American press showed little interest in this victory for democracy. Howells wrote him on December 29, 1889:

> I have just heated myself up with your righteous wrath about our indifference to the Brazilian republic. But it seems to me that you ignore the real reason for it, which is that there is no longer any American republic, but an aristocracy-loving oligarchy in place of it. Why should our money-bags rejoice in the explosion of a wind-bag? They know at the bottom of the holes where their

> souls ought to be that if such an event finally means anything, it means *their* ruin next; and so they *don't* rejoice; and as *they* mostly inspire the people's voice—the press—the press is dumb.[91]

The novel's illustrator, Daniel Carter Beard, had given a slave-driver the face of the robber baron Jay Gould.

That Howells's sympathies were by no means confined to the local scene is evidenced by his scorn for America's role in the Spanish-American War. A national conference on social reform, meeting in June 1898, in Buffalo, adopted this declaration: "Militarism, expressed in our war of conquest in the Philippines, is but the offspring and incident of the greater menace of plutocracy, which has established monopoly government in place of government by the people."[92] Howells was one of the sponsors of the conference; among the others were Jane Addams, Booker T. Washington, Henry Demarest Lloyd, and Edwin D. Mead.

Howells saw through the jingoistic rhetoric of the war to the real nature of America's "imperialist grab." (John Hay, ambassador to Great Britain, told Theodore Roosevelt that it was "a splendid little war."[93]) Howells wrote Henry James on July 31: "We are in sight of peace. Our war for humanity has unmasked itself as a war for coaling stations, and we are going to keep our booty to punish Spain for putting us to the trouble of using violence in robbing her."[94]

In a letter to his sister Aurelia on July 4, 1916, four months after President Woodrow Wilson had sent troops to Mexico in pursuit of Pancho Villa's forces, Howells said: "The possibility of war with Mexico is dreadful, and is the effect of Wilson's folly.... This is wickeder than the old Mexican War of 1846, which Father so abhorred, and more stupid and objectless."[95]

Several months earlier, he had expressed his horror at the execution of the Irish Marxist James Connolly and thirteen of his captured comrades, following the Easter Rising. In a letter that appeared in the *New York Evening Post* on May 6 and was reprinted in the *Nation* on May 18, he wrote:

> Nothing more lamentable in the course of the war now raging has come to pass than this act of bloody vengeance by the English government.... The shooting of the Irish insurrectionists is too much like the shooting of prisoners of war, too much like taking a leaf from the German classic of *Schrecklichkeit* [terror]; and in giving way to her vengeance, England has roused the moral sense of mankind against her."[96]

On June 16, 1916, Howells wrote about the Haymarket case once more. Waldo R. Browne, the son of Francis Fisher Browne, was preparing a biography of John Peter Altgeld and had asked Howells for his recollections. He replied: "I met him only once, at [Jane Addams's] Hull House [in Chicago, in 1899], and had the joy of telling him how glad of him I was."[97]

Howells's death on May 11, 1920, at the age of eighty-three, was marked by the *New York Times* with a lengthy editorial lauding him for his charm, geniality, and versatility, and calling him "the most distinguished purely American literary figure of his time."[98] But the *Times* entirely failed to mention Howells's social concerns—his deep sympathy with working people, his interest in Socialism, his condemnation of imperialism, his efforts to promote racial equality, and his valiant stand on behalf of the Haymarket martyrs.

It frequently happens that a person's radicalism, once he is dead and unable to defend himself, is publicly ignored, and an acceptable stereotype is substituted. The myth of a bland Howells has all too often been presented without being challenged. His mature awareness and literary achievement—and, above all, his criticism of society—have generally been ignored or minimized.

The conventional wisdom was accepted even by such a liberal as Matthew Josephson, who, surprisingly, failed to gauge the depth and intensity of Howells's involvement in the Haymarket case and other causes, and his genuine valor. Josephson diminished both Howells and the events of the time by writing, in *Portrait of the Artist as American*, "True, during the Haymarket riots of Chicago in 1887 [*sic*], when the press and the whole country called for the blood of the seven Anarchists, Howells did write a letter of beautiful indignation to the governor of Illinois, but no preachers or authors, from either Boston or New York, followed him in his cause, and the fruitless effort was speedily hushed up."

Equally groundless is Josephson's assertion: "Generous and kind as he could be, Howells wrote from no depth of conviction; he celebrated or attacked no institution with a fixed moral passion.... When we compare the realists and social critics of Howells's type to great Europeans who had been attacking society for two centuries, we become painfully aware of their timidity."[99]

What Josephson failed to understand is that Howells should be compared not with "great Europeans" but with his American contemporaries. By such a measure, he stands out as a person of courage and conscience, an example who prompted Eleanor Marx to salute him as "a brave and just man."

A Personal Postscript

In the course of my research I went to visit the novelist's grandson Dr. William White Howells, professor of anthropology at Harvard University, in the spring of 1978. (His father, John Mead Howells, an architect, had designed Mark Twain's home, Stormfield, built in Redding, Connecticut, in 1908.)

In 1909 the novelist had sent his older grandson a card on his first St. Valentine's Day. I asked Dr. Howells whether he still possessed it. He ruefully admitted that he did not. It appears in Mildred Howells's edition of her father's letters:

> Dear little Child whose count of days
> Is of like number with my years,
> I have but rounded on my ways
> And in your start my goal appears.
>
> My hopes have been what yours shall be,
> Your joys to come in turn were mine;
> May the same love in you and me
> Keep us each other's Valentine.

And on his seventy-second birthday, March 1, 1909, Howells sent this note to his grandson:

> Dear Billy:
>
> It was very sweet of you to send that birthday card, where we are walking toward the sunset

together. It is a lovely sunset, but sad, and the night is beyond it. Hold fast to my hand, dear little boy, and keep me with you as long as you can. Someday, I hope not too late, you will know how I love you.

Your aff'te grandfather,
W. D. Howells[100]

As we chatted in his office, Professor Howells, who was eleven years old when his grandfather died, seemed bemused by my interest in his involvement in the Haymarket affair. "He was quite a good businessman," he said (true enough, Howells knew how to negotiate with publishers and to protect his rights as an author), "and my grandmother was a peppery little lady." He added, "You know, Anarchism was not his cup of tea."

I did not think the time or place appropriate for disputation, but I promised to send him a copy of my essay. I did observe, however, as I took leave of the professor, that his grandfather was a man of generous impulses, a believer in justice, a courageous man—and that is why I considered it important to bring this aspect of his life out of obscurity.

Appendix A

Facsimile of the Letter from Eleanor Marx to William Dean Howells

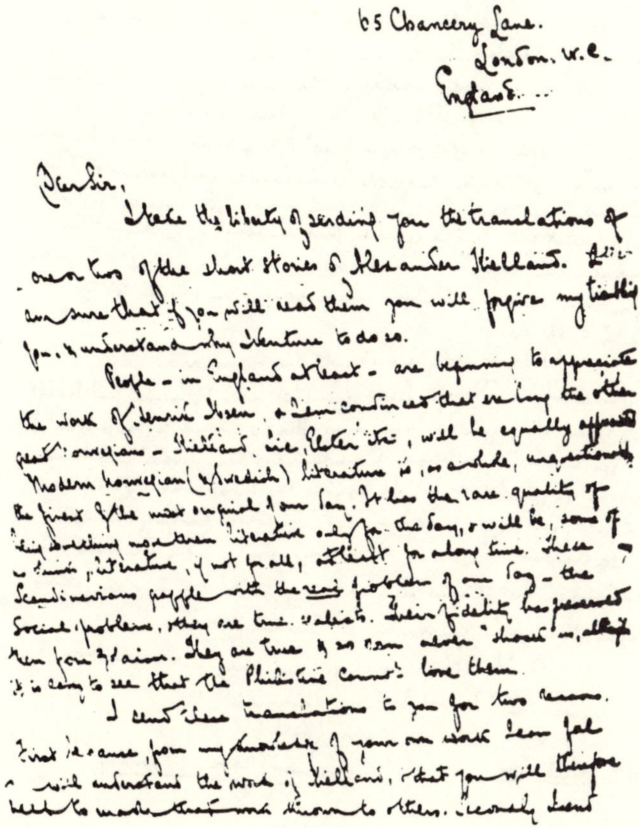

65 Chancery Lane.
London. W.C.
England...

Dear Sir,

I take the liberty of sending you the translations of one or two of the short stories of Alexander Kielland. I am sure that if you will read them you will forgive my troubling you, & understand why I venture to do so.

People – in England at least – are beginning to appreciate the work of Henrik Ibsen, & I am convinced that sooner or later the other great Norwegians – Kielland, Lie, Elster etc, will be equally appreciated. Modern Norwegian (& Swedish) literature is, as a whole, unquestionably the finest & the most original of our day. It has the rare quality of being something more than literature only for the day, & will be, some of it, literature, if not for all, at least for a long time. These Scandinavians grapple with the real problems of our day – the social problems, they are true realists. Their fidelity has prevented [illegible]. They are true & so [illegible] It is easy to see that the Philistines cannot love them.

I send these translations to you for two reasons. First because, from my knowledge of your own work I am sure you will understand the work of Kielland, & that you will therefore help to make that work known to others. Secondly I send to you because ever since you had the courage to sign the appeal demanding a new trial for the Anarchists, I have known you were not only a true artist & a great writer, but that even rarer thing, a brave & just man. All you have written of late, & the way in which you speak of the "unnecessary suffering" of the great mass of humanity tell me you feel with the people, & must therefore understand how Kielland loves them. Kielland's work is not "in a sense" didactic. It is perfect art but he teaches great lessons. I think, the making such work known is also good work. If you feel this, perhaps you will recommend these strange Norwegian stories to the Editor of Harper's.

Now one egotistic word as to the translator. I have Englished Ibsen's "Enemy of Society" (Camelot Series) & have just translated his latest play with his permission. This is about to be published by Fisher Unwin. I have translated other works: "Madame Bovary" (if you'd honour me by reading my Introduction to that work I'd gladly send it to you), & Lissagaray's "Histoire de la Commune".

For the rest you may know my name. My husband & I lectured in the States in 1886 on Socialism — & my father's name I am sure you know. — Karl Marx.

I trust you will excuse my writing in this informal way. Indeed I know you will!

Yours faithfully
Eleanor Marx-Aveling

W. D. Howells Esq.

65 Chancery Lane
London, W.C.
England

Dear Sir,

I take the liberty of sending you the translations of one or two of the short stories of Alexander Kielland. I am sure that if you will read them you will forgive my troubling you, and understand why I venture to do so.

People—in England at least—are beginning to appreciate the work of Henrik Ibsen and I am convinced that ere long the other great Norwegians—Kielland, Lie, Elster, etc., will be equally appreciated. Modern Norwegian (and Swedish) literature is, as a whole, unquestionably the finest and the most original of our day. It has the rare quality of being something more than literature only for the day, and will be, some of us think, literature if not for all, at least for a long time. These Scandinavians grapple with the *real* problem of our day—the social problem; they are true Realists. Their fidelity has preserved them from Zolaism. They are true and can never "shock" us although it is easy to see that the Philistine cannot love them.

I send these translations to you for two reasons. First, because from my knowledge of your own work I can feel you will understand the work of Kielland, and that you will therefore help to make that work known to others. Secondly, I send them to you because ever since you had the courage to sign the appeal demanding a new trial for the Anarchists, I have known you were not only a true artist and a great writer, but that even rarer thing, a brave and just man. All you have written of late, and the way in which you speak of the *unnecessary* suffering of the great mass of humanity, tell me you feel with the people and must therefore understand how Kielland loves them. Kielland's work is not in a sense "didactic." It is perfect art. But he teaches great lessons. I think the making such work known is also good work. If you feel this perhaps you will recommend these strange Norwegian stories to the Editor of *Harper's*.

Now one egotistic word as to the translator. I have Englished Ibsen's *Enemy of Society* [*An Enemy of the People*] (Camelot Series) and have just translated his latest play with his permission. This is about to be published, by Fisher Unwin. I have translated other works: *Madame Bovary* (if you would honor me by reading my introduction to that work I would gladly send it to you), and Lissagaray's *Histoire de la Commune*.

For the rest you may know my name. My husband and I lectured in the States in 1886 on Socialism, and my father's name I am sure you know—Karl Marx.

I trust you will excuse my writing in this informal way. Indeed I know you will.

Yours faithfully
Eleanor Marx-Aveling

W. D. Howells, Esq.

Appendix B

Facsimile of the Letter from August Spies, Michael Schwab, and Samuel Fielden to Governor Richard J. Oglesby

Chicago, Nov. 3. '87

Governor Rich. Oglesby
Springfield, Ill.

Sir:

In order that the truth may be known by you, and the public you represent, we desire to state that we never advocated the use of force, except in cases of selfdefense. To accuse us of having attempted to overthrow law and government on May 4. '86, or at any other time, is as false as it is absurd. What ever we said or did was said and done publicly; we have never conspired or plotted to commit an unlawful act. While we attacked the present social arrangements in writing and speech, and exposed their iniquities, we have never consciously broken any laws. So far from having planned the killing of anybody at the Haymarket, the very object of the meeting was to protest against the commission of murder! All our efforts have been in the direction to elevate mankind, and to remove as much as possible the causes of crime in society. Our labor was unselfish; no motive of personal gain or ambition prompted us. Thousands and thousands will bear testimony to this. We may have erred at times in our judgement—yes, we may have "loved mankind not wisely, but too well". —

Yours respectfully
A. Spies Michael Schwab S. Fielden

Appendix C

Facsimile of the Letter from August Spies to William M. Salter

Thursday, Nov. 3. 87

My Dear Mr Salter:—

Captain Black
has written an appeal to the governor,
signed by some of us, which contains
essentially the same statements. Whether
under the circumstances it is wise to
present the letter I enclose in this also,
this you may desire. I think it would be
as well if you would simply explain to the
governor orally anything that he does
not seem to understand. I am, as a matter
of course, sorry for the poor devils who lost
their lives at the Haymarket, but I am
more so for the lives of the poor
devils who perished on the previous
day. Who cares for their wretched families?
Nobody. Now, for me to express condolence
over the killing of the policemen, and
not at the same time over that of the
poor fellows at McCormicks or at East
St Louis, would be an act of hypocrisy,

2/

such as I would not be guilty
of under any circumstances. suffice
it to say, that I abhor murder
in *every* form. If I did not I
would never have become a
socialist!

Whether or not to make use
of the accompanying letter, I leave
entirely to your good judgement.
Thanking you for the kind interest
you have taken in our case, I
am Yours very truly

[illegible]

[illegible]

Appendix D

Facsimile of the Telegram from William M. Salter to William Dean Howells on the Eve of the Executions

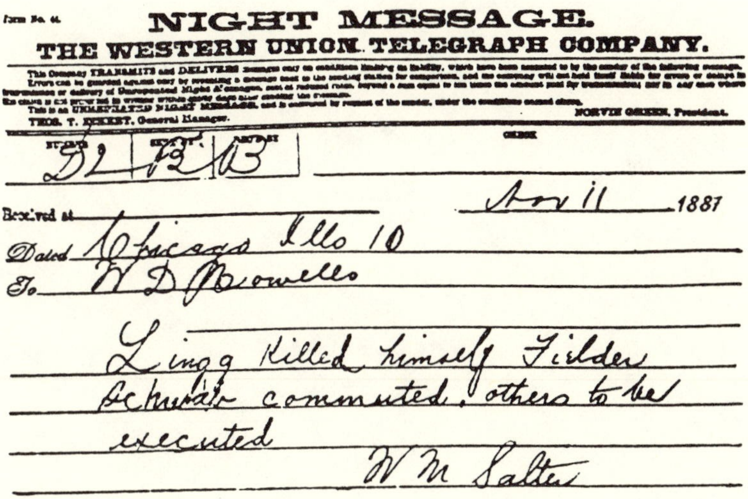

NIGHT MESSAGE.

THE WESTERN UNION TELEGRAPH COMPANY.

NORVIN GREEN, President.

THOS. T. ECKERT, General Manager.

Nov 11 1887

Received at

Dated Chicago Ills 10

To W D Howells

Lingg killed himself Fielden Schwab commuted. others to be executed

W M Salter

Appendix E

The Haymarket Defendants

Albert R. Parsons was born in Montgomery, Alabama, on June 20, 1848, the youngest of ten children. "My ancestry," he wrote while imprisoned, "goes back to the earliest settlers in this country, the first Parsons family landing on the shores of Narragansett Bay, from England, in 1632."[101] His father was from Maine, his mother from New Jersey. She died when he was not yet two years old, and when he was four his father died. He was raised by his oldest brother, William, in Tyler, Texas. When the Civil War began, he was an apprentice typesetter on the *Galveston Daily News.* Though only thirteen years old, he joined a Confederate infantry regiment, and later he served as a cavalry scout, under William's command, until the war's end.

After returning home, both brothers became supporters of Reconstruction, in response to the indignities they saw being inflicted on black people. Albert bought a small farm, and with the money from his first crop of corn he attended Waco (now Baylor) University for a term. In 1866, the Republicans gained control of Texas politics, and he began to work for the office of the district clerk, traveling from town to town encouraging black people to vote. He published a newspaper, the *Waco Spectator*, from 1867 to 1868, and then was a roving correspondent for William's newspaper, the *Houston Telegraph.* From 1870 to 1873, he served as assistant assessor, and later chief deputy collector, for the U.S. Internal Revenue Service; as secretary of the Texas State Senate, of which William was a member; and as an officer in the state militia, often protecting black citizens from racial violence.

In 1873, when the Democrats regained control of Texas and ended Reconstruction, he became a free-lance journalist and traveled north, settling in Chicago. (The brothers met again in 1886, when William, now a judge in Texas, came to Chicago to lend his support to the defendants.) He worked as a compositor on the *Chicago Inter-Ocean* and the *Chicago Times.* The depression of 1873–1879 and the 1877 rail strike, as well as the other labor struggles of the era, made him a Socialist. He became known in Chicago and elsewhere as a stirring speaker, and between 1877 and 1882 he frequently ran for local office. As a representative of the typographical union, he was one of the founders of the Chicago Trades and Labor Council in 1878. From 1878 to 1879, he was associate editor of the *Socialist*, and in 1884 he began his own paper, the *Alarm.* At the time of his arrest, he was thirty-seven years old and was the father of two children.

His wife, Lucy Eldine González Parsons, was born in Texas about 1853 of black, Indian, and Spanish ancestry. When her husband was condemned to death, she embarked on a national tour to tell the true story of Haymarket. Later she spoke in England, where William Morris, George Bernard Shaw, and others had taken up the cause of the defendants. In 1889, she wrote *The Life of Albert Parsons* and published it herself. At the annual commemoration in Waldheim Cemetery she was the leading speaker, and over the years she addressed many other political gatherings. In 1905 she attended the founding convention of the Industrial Workers of the World. She joined the Communist Party in 1939. On March 7, 1942, she died in a fire at her home in Chicago. She is buried near her husband.

August Spies was born in Landeck, Germany, on December 10, 1855. His father, a government forester, died when he was seventeen, and he was forced to leave school, where he had been studying for the same occupation. Later that year he emigrated to the United States. He learned the craft of upholstery in New York City and in 1873 settled in Chicago, where he opened his own shop in 1876. He was so successful that he was able to bring his mother, his sister, and his three brothers from Germany. But after hearing a lecture on Socialism in 1875 and reading Marx's *Capital*, he became a Socialist. During the 1877 rail strike he gained prominence as a speaker, and that year he ran for local office. In 1884 he began working as the editor of the *Arbeiter-Zeitung*. He was thirty years old at the time of his arrest.

Nina Van Zandt, the twenty-five-year-old daughter of a Chicago pharmaceuticals manufacturer, and a graduate of Vassar College, attended the trial and visited Spies in the Cook County Jail. On January 29, 1887, they were married. Henry Spies took the vows as proxy for his brother, since the sheriff refused to allow the wedding to be held in the jail. She and her parents were reviled in the press, and their home was attacked by a mob. Later that year, she published *August Spies's Autobiography*, which they had worked on together. (His mother, Christine, published it in German in 1888.) She spoke at the annual memorial ceremony for the martyrs and attended many other political events. She was twice remarried. In 1936, she died in Chicago, poverty-striken; it is said that when she married Spies, she and her parents were cut out of an aunt's will, losing a bequest of four hundred thousand dollars. Lucy Parsons spoke at her funeral. She is buried close to Spies's grave.

Samuel Fielden was born in the town of Todmorden, in Lancashire, England, on February 25, 1847. His father, a weaver, was a Chartist who fought for the eight-hour day; his mother, who died when he was ten, was a Methodist. At the age of eight, he went to work in the same cotton mill as his father. As a young man, he became known locally as a lay preacher and a political orator. He heard a group of black people from America who made a lecture tour of Lancashire before the Civil War, and his first political speech was a denunciation of slavery. He emigrated to the United States when he was twenty-one years old.

Like every one of the seven Haymarket defendants who had come from other countries, he was radicalized by the shock of finding here the same kind of economic injustice as in his native land. He worked in a textile mill in Providence, Rhode Island; on a farm in Illinois; as a day laborer on the Illinois and Michigan Canal; and, for six years, as a stone-hauler in Chicago, where he was one of the founders of the first teamsters' union, in 1880. At the time of his arrest, he was thirty-nine years old and was the father of two children. After he was pardoned, he used a small inheritance to buy a ranch near La Veta, Colorado, the town where Lizzie and William Holmes were living. He died there in 1922 and is the only Haymarket defendant not buried in Waldheim Cemetery.

Adolph Fischer was born in Bremen, Germany, in 1858. He was introduced to Socialism by his father. (The father's occupation is not known, but he was prosperous enough to give his son eight and a half years of schooling.) At the age of fifteen, he emigrated to the United States, joining his brother William in Little Rock, Arkansas. After serving his apprenticeship on William's German-language newspaper, he worked in St. Louis and other cities. In 1883, he settled in Chicago and became a compositor on the *Arbeiter-Zeitung*. He and George Engel founded the *Anarchist*, a monthly, in January 1886, and published four issues. At the time of his arrest, he was twenty-eight years old and was the father of three children.

George Engel was born in Kassel, Germany, on April 15, 1836. His father, a bricklayer, died when he was eighteen months old; his mother died when he was eleven. He was so poor that he could not obtain an apprenticeship, until he met a kindly painter in Frankfurt who agreed to teach him. When he had learned his craft, he traveled from place to place working as a painter. But mechanization made work hard to find, and in 1873 he emigrated to the United States. In Philadelphia he worked in a sugar factory, until his health broke down. After recovering, he moved to Chicago, where he worked in a wagon factory and as a painter. He was introduced to Socialism by a fellow worker. In 1876, he was able to open a toy shop, which he ran with his wife and daughter. "As a shopkeeper," he explained, "I had more time which I could devote to reading."[102] He also published the *Anarchist*, with George Engel, in 1886. He was fifty years old at the time of his arrest.

Michael Schwab was born on August 9, 1853, in the town of Kitzingen, in Bavaria, Germany. His mother died when he was eight; his father, a small tradesman, died when he was twelve. After serving an apprenticeship as a bookbinder, he worked in Germany, Austria, and Switzerland. It was during these years that he became a union member and a Socialist. He emigrated to the United States in 1879, settled in Chicago, and two years later became associate editor of the *Arbeiter-Zeitung.* At the time of his arrest, he was thirty-two years old and was the father of two children. After he was pardoned, he resumed his work on the *Arbeiter-Zeitung.* In 1895 he opened a shoe store in which he also sold books. Three years later, he died of tuberculosis.

Oscar Neebe was born of German parents in New York City on July 12, 1850, but he spent his childhood in the state of Hesse-Kassel, Germany. When he was fourteen, his parents returned to New York. There, and in Philadelphia and Chicago, he was a factory worker, a waiter, a cook on a ship, a tinsmith, a yeast salesman, and a partner, with his brother, in a small yeast company. The rail strike of 1877 served as his introduction to the labor movement, and he became active in the brewers' and bakers' unions. At the time of his arrest, he was thirty-five years old and was the father of three children. After he was pardoned, he married again (his first wife had died during his imprisonment), helped his wife run the tavern she owned, and resumed his union-organizing. He was a delegate to the 1907 convention of the Industrial Workers of the World. In 1916 he died.

Louis Lingg was born in the town of Schwetzingen, in Baden, Germany, on September 9, 1864. When he was ten, his father, a lumber worker, was injured at work and dismissed from his job; he was an invalid until his death three years later. His mother struggled to support the family as a laundress. After he completed his apprenticeship as a carpenter, he worked in Germany and Switzerland from 1882 until 1885, when he emigrated to the United States. In Chicago, he worked as a carpenter and then was hired as an organizer by the International Carpenters' and Joiners' Union. At the time of his arrest, he was twenty-eight years old. About his death, William J. Adelman writes, in *Haymarket Revisited*: "The Neebe family always believed that the police gave him [Lingg] a cigar that morning with a dynamite cap in it, since, by November 10, 1887, the public attitude was beginning to change toward the executions. His supposed suicide was used to propagandize the guilt of the other four."[103] And when I interviewed Lucy Parsons in 1934, she told me that she was convinced the police were implicated in Lingg's death.

References*

Preface

1. Reed, "The IWW in Court," *Liberator*, September 1918; reprinted in *The Education of John Reed*, p. 181.
2. Alger, "The Literature of Exposure," *Atlantic Monthly*, August 1905, pp. 210–211.
3. Schluter, *Lincoln, Labor, and Slavery*, pp. 171–173, 175–177.

John Swinton, Crusading Editor

1. Waters, *Career and Conversation of John Swinton*, pp. 8, 9, 11, 16, 18.
2. Debs, *John Swinton, Radical Editor and Leader*, p. 51.
3. Berger, *The Story of the "New York Times,"* pp. 250–251.
4. O'Brien, *The Story of the "Sun,"* p. 233.

*For a complete listing of all the works cited in the References, as well as suggestions for further reading, see the Bibliography.

5. Maverick, *Henry J. Raymond and the New York Press*, p. 353.

6. Hough, *The Quiet Rebel*, p. 23.

7. Twain and Howells, *Mark Twain–Howells Letters*, Vol. 2, p. 581.

8. Calmer, *Labor Agitator*, p. 115.

9. Ely, *Ground Under Our Feet*, p. 66.

10. Waters, *Career and Conversation of John Swinton*, p. 31.

11. Marx and Engels, *Letters to Americans*, pp. 121–123, 124, 127.

12. Foner, "Protests in the United States Against Bismarck's Anti-Socialist Law," p. 31.

13. Foner, *When Karl Marx Died*, pp. 83, 94, 97–98.

14. Foner, *History of the Labor Movement in the United States*, Vol. 2, p. 63.

15. Ross, "John Swinton," pp. 69–70.

16. Waters, *Career and Conversation of John Swinton*, p. 24.

17. Perlman, "John Swinton," p. 491.

18. Debs, "John Swinton, Radical Editor and Leader," p. 32.

19. Sinclair, *The Cry for Justice*, p. 428.

20. Ross, "John Swinton," pp. 111–112.

21. Swinton, "Lincoln, 1860—Debs, 1894," reprinted in Debs, *Life, Writings, and Speeches*, p. 504.

22. Debs, *John Swinton, Radical Editor and Leader*, pp. 45, 46, 49, 50.
23. Swinton, *Striking for Life*, p. 29.
24. Swinton, letter to the *New York Herald*, April 11, 1876, in Holloway, *Whitman*, pp. 206–207.
25. Traubel, *With Walt Whitman in Camden*, Vol. 2, pp. 339–340.
26. Allen, *The Solitary Singer*, p. 400.
27. Whitman, *The Correspondence*, Vol. 3, pp. 38–39.
28. Stepanchev, "Whitman in Russia," p. 145.
29. Traubel, *With Walt Whitman in Camden*, Vol. 2, pp. 271, 393.
30. Traubel, *With Walt Whitman in Camden*, Vol. 1, pp. 23–25. (*The Correspondence of Walt Whitman* corrects 1884, the date given by Traubel, to 1874.)
31. Swinton, *Striking for Life*, pp. 287–289.

Charles P. Steinmetz, Scientist and Socialist

1. *Boston Globe*, January 12, 1917.
2. Hart, *Schenectady and the Golden Era*, p. 20.
3. Joseph Baker, in *Scientific American*, May 6, 1911.
4. Nonetheless, Steinmetz is listed in the *Standard Jewish Encyclopedia*, the *Universal Jewish Encyclopedia*, and the *Encyclopedia Judaica*.
5. Hammond, *Charles Proteus Steinmetz*, pp. 8, 9.
6. Coleman, "Charles P. Steinmetz," in *Pioneers of Freedom*, p. 265.

7. E. W. Rice, in *Science*, November 16, 1923.
8. Broderick, *Steinmetz and His Discoverer*, p. 14.
9. Steinmetz, "Socialism and Invention," *Review of Reviews*, January 1920.
10. A Columbia University sociologist, Bernhard J. Stern (1894–1956), contended that capitalism acts as a brake on scientific initiative. Dr. Stern, a Marxist scholar, cited the "shelving" of patents by giant corporations for the purpose of stifling competition. Many technological innovations have been suppressed, he argued, "because changes may disturb profits." (See "The Frustrations of Technology," in *Science and Society*, Winter 1937.)
11. Steinmetz, in the *American*, May 1918.
12. Clyde Wagoner, in the *Schenectady Indian*, July 1950.
13. George R. Lunn (1873–1948), a native of Iowa, came to Schenectady as pastor of the First Dutch Reformed Church in 1904. His sermons, attacking national as well as local evils, brought him increasing attention and led to his nomination for mayor.
14. Bibber, *Charles Proteus Steinmetz*, pp. 13–14.
15. Bibber, *Charles Proteus Steinmetz*, p. 14.
16. Coleman, "Charles P. Steinmetz," in *Pioneers of Freedom*, p. 218.
17. Weinstein, *The Decline of Socialism in America*, p. 109.
18. Walter Lippmann (1889–1974), author and political commentator, was a Harvard classmate of John Reed's and a founding editor of the *New Republic*. During World War I, he was an assistant to Secretary of War

Newton D. Baker and then a captain in U.S. military intelligence. Later he became an editorial-writer on the *New York World* and a syndicated columnist on the *New York Herald Tribune.*

19. Morris Hillquit (1870–1933), a lawyer, was a leader and theoretician of the Socialist Party, a member of its national executive committee, and for many years its representative at international conferences. Hillquit, in his autobiography, *Loose Leaves from a Busy Life*, says that Lippmann served in the Lunn administration for two years; in fact, it was four months.
20. Lippmann, *A Preface to Politics*, p. 183.
21. *New York Call*, June 1912.
22. *Masses*, April 1912.
23. Winter and Hicks, *The Letters of Lincoln Steffens*, Vol. 2, p. 908.
24. Johnson, *The Letters of William Allen White*, p. 324.
25. State of New York, *Proceedings of the Judiciary Committee of the Assembly*, Vol. 1, pp. 352–366.
26. *New Review*, December 1914.
27. The symposium appeared in the June 1, 1915, issue of the *New Review.* Contributors included Eugene V. Debs, Gustavus Myers, Rose Pastor Stokes, and Robert H. Lowie. The general tenor was expressed by Debs, who said, "Prussian militarism has gone stark mad."
28. Hawley B. Van Vechten (1885–1960) was editor of the Socialist *Schenectady Citizen* from 1917 to 1936 and served as city clerk from 1912 to 1913. The Van Vechten Papers are at the Schenectady City History Center.

29. Bailey and Ryan, *The "Lusitania" Disaster*, pp. 96, 233.

30. Robert M. La Follette, Sr. (1855–1925), represented the state of Wisconsin in the U.S. Senate for many years. He fought the trusts and monopolies on behalf of farmers and small businesses. His St. Paul speech (*La Follette*, Vol. 2, p. 767) precipitated a campaign of vilification and an attempt to expel him from the Senate. (These events are described in *La Follette*, by his wife, Belle Case La Follette, and his daughter, Fola La Follette, but are omitted from Allan Nevins's foreword to the 1968 edition of La Follette's 1913 *Autobiography*.)

31. *Fort Wayne* (Indiana) *Journal-Gazette*, May 24, 1917.

32. Syndicated article, National Enterprise Association, October 13, 1922.

33. Published in the Soviet press, April 19, 1922. The present letter is from Anikeyev and Solovyov, *Lenin Through the Eyes of the World*. Steinmetz's letter and Lenin's reply also appeared in the foreign-relations section of the *Nation*, July 19, 1922.

34. Gleb Maximilian Krzhizhanovsky (1872–1959) became head of the State Commission for Electrification in 1920, at Lenin's suggestion.

35. Ludwig Karlovich Martens (1875–1948), a prominent engineer, was the Soviet representative in the United States from 1919 to 1921. He tried to normalize relations between the two countries but was expelled from the U.S. and returned to Soviet Russia, where he served on the Presidium of the Supreme Economic Council.

36. Lenin, *Collected Works*, Vol. 35, pp. 552–553; first published in *Pravda*, April 19, 1922.

37. Lenin, *Collected Works*, Vol. 31, p. 516.

38. Harold M. Ware (1892–1935), an American agronomist and Communist, was the son of Ella Reeve ("Mother") Bloor, a leader of the Communist Party. He went to Soviet Russia in 1922 as the head of a tractor brigade that he had organized in the United States. The twenty-four tractors that he brought had been purchased with funds contributed by Americans who were sympathetic to Soviet reconstruction. The brigade worked on the Toikino State Farm, in Perm Gubernia. Lenin praised the American volunteers in a message to the Presidium of the All-Russian Central Executive Committee on October 24, 1922.

39. Lenin, *Collected Works*, Vol. 45, p. 597; first published in English in *Soviet Russia Pictorial*, July 1923.

40. *Soviet Russia Pictorial*, July 1923.

41. *Lenin on the United States*, p. 578.

42. Jessica Smith, in *New World Review*, Winter 1970; reprinted in *Lenin's Impact on the United States* (New York: New World Review, 1970).

43. The Russian-American Industrial Corporation was organized by the Amalgamated Clothing Workers of America, on the initiative of its president, Sidney Hillman. Incorporated with capitalization of $1,000,000, the RAIC sold stock at $10 a share. It worked jointly with the Supreme Economic Council of Soviet Russia in operating nineteen clothing factories in Moscow, an equal number in Petrograd (later renamed Leningrad), and eight in Kazan.

44. *Soviet Russia*, December 1922.

45. Americans involved in the Kuzbas project included the former general secretary of the Industrial Workers of the World (IWW), William D. ("Big Bill") Haywood, and Bill Shatoff, a leading member of the IWW.

46. In 1927, Maurer was a member of the first trade-union delegation to the USSR. Among the others were Paul H. Douglas, professor of economics at the University of Chicago and later a Democratic U.S. senator from Illinois; Rexford G. Tugwell, professor of economics at Columbia University and later a member of President Franklin Delano Roosevelt's "brain trust"; and Robert W. Dunn, director of the Labor Research Association.

47. *New York Times*, July 2, 1923.

48. *Nation*, January 3, 1923.

49. *New York Times*, July 2, 1923.

50. *Soviet Russia Pictorial*, July 1923.

51. Steinmetz is listed in another lunatic-fringe volume, *The Red Network* (1934), with such other "reds" as Roger N. Baldwin, Felix Frankfurter, Albert Einstein, and Mahatma Gandhi.

52. Hammond, *Charles Proteus Steinmetz*, pp. 19, 20.

53. Abraham A. Heller (1874–1962) was a businessman and a friend of the Soviet Union. He assisted financially in the establishment of International Publishers in 1924 and for a number of years took an active part in its operations. Memorial tributes were written by Otto Nathan (*National Guardian*, October 8, 1962) and Arnold Johnson (*Worker*, November 6, 1962).

54. In the preface to his book, Heller acknowledged the help of "A. C. Freeman." This was the pseudonym of William Henry Chamberlin (1897–1969), a *Christian Science Monitor* correspondent in the USSR (1922–1934) and in the Far East and Europe (1934–1940). In his memoir *The Confessions of an Individualist* (1941), he boasted that he wrote as "A. C. Freeman" only for radical publications. He capped his career with the anti-Soviet book *Russia's Iron Age* and as a columnist for the *Wall Street Journal* and the *New Leader.*

55. "The Place of Religion in Modern Scientific Civilization." Address delivered by Steinmetz on Laymen's Sunday, November 5, 1922, at All Souls' Church, Schenectady. Published as *Bulletin* No. 11 by the Unitarian Laymen's League, 7 Park Square, Boston.

56. Claessens, *Didn't We Have Fun!* pp. 13, 14.

57. *New York Times*, October 15, 1923.

58. *Schenectady Gazette*, October 18, 1923.

59. *New York Times*, November 1, 1923.

60. *New York Times*, October 29, 1923.

61. Vladimir Karapetoff (1876–1948) was a professor of electrical engineering at Cornell University. Born in St. Petersburg, he was sent to this country by the tsarist government as an engineering apprentice and decided to remain here. Prior to joining the Cornell faculty he was employed by the Westinghouse Electric Company. He invented many electrical devices, wrote textbooks, and was a consultant to industrial firms. He was also a prominent member of the Socialist Party. In addition, he wrote a volume of poems, developed a cello with five

strings, and gave piano recitals throughout the United States. He became blind in 1943 but remained active as a teacher, Socialist, and musician until his death.

62. *Cornell Daily Sun*, October 29, 1923.
63. *New York Times*, November 1, 1923.
64. *New York Times*, October 27, 1923.
65. Interview with Joseph Hayden, October 21, 1976.
66. *GE News*, April 16, 1965.
67. Interview with Celia Rhein, October 21, 1976.
68. Telephone conversation with Celia Rhein, November 14, 1976.
69. *Albany Evening News*, December 14, 1925.
70. General Electric Company, *Annual Report, 1923*.
71. "Steinmetz was the most valuable piece of apparatus General Electric had, until he wore out and died." (John Dos Passos, *The Forty-Second Parallel* [Part 1 of *U.S.A.*])
72. Matles and Higgins, *Them and Us*, pp. 82, 83.

William Dean Howells and the Haymarket Era

1. Calmer, *Labor Agitator*, p. 124.
2. Kapp, *Eleanor Marx*, Vol. 2, p. 161.
3. Cady, *The Realist at War*, p. 157.
4. Stidger, *Edwin Markham*, p. 136.
5. Peck, *The Personal Equation*, p. 13.
6. Altgeld, *The Mind and Spirit of John Peter Altgeld*, pp. 94–95.

7. Myers, *History of the Great American Fortunes*, Vol. 2, p. 230.
8. Lloyd, *Henry Demarest Lloyd*, Vol. 1, p. 85.
9. Dombrowski, *The Early Years of Christian Socialism*, p. 129.
10. Lovett, *All Our Years*, p. 55.
11. Avrich, *The Haymarket Tragedy*, p. 287.
12. Howells, *Life in Letters*, Vol. 1, p. 398.
13. Howells, *Selected Letters*, Vol. 3, pp. 197–198.
14. Whittier, *The Letters of John Greenleaf Whittier*, Vol. 3, p. 538.
15. Howells, *Selected Letters*, Vol. 3, p. 198.
16. Carter, "The Haymarket Affair in Literature," p. 270.
17. Howells, *Selected Letters*, Vol. 3, pp. 193, 194.
18. Kirk and Kirk, "William Dean Howells, George William Curtis, and the Haymarket Affair," pp. 494–496.
19. Howells, *Life in Letters*, Vol. 1, pp. 398–399.
20. David, *The History of the Haymarket Affair*, p. 14.
21. Becker, "William Dean Howells," pp. 283–291.
22. Lynn, *William Dean Howells*, p. 291.
23. David, *The History of the Haymarket Affair*, p. 395.
24. Morris, *The Collected Letters*, Vol. 2, pp. 706, 707.
25. Avrich, *Anarchist Portraits*, p. 80.
26. Young, *Life and Times*, p. 108.
27. Thompson, *William Morris*, p. 487.

28. David, *The History of the Haymarket Affair*, pp. 428–429.
29. Tebbel, *An American Dynasty*, p. 53.
30. Gutman, "Workers Search for Power," p. 38.
31. Tebbel, *An American Dynasty*, p. 54.
32. Pringle, *Theodore Roosevelt*, pp. 110–111.
33. David, *The History of the Haymarket Affair*, p. 10.
34. Powderly, *Thirty Years of Labor*, p. 543.
35. Fine, *Labor and Farmer Parties in the United States*, p. 53.
36. *John Swinton's Paper*, August 22, 1886.
37. Goldman, *Living My Life*, Vol. 1, p. 10.
38. David, *The History of the Haymarket Affair*, p. 412.
39. Young, *Life and Times*, p. 108.
40. Wilson, "William Dean Howells's Unpublished Letters About the Haymarket Affair," pp. 5–19.
41. David, *The History of the Haymarket Affair*, p. 399.
42. This letter, and those cited below under the designation "Knox College," were for many years restricted for publication. They are in the Memorabilia Room of the Knox College Library, Galesburg, Illinois.
43. Knox College.
44. Knox College.
45. Knox College.
46. Ward, "Another Howells Anarchist Letter," pp. 489–490.

47. Howells, *Selected Letters*, Vol. 3, p. 200.

48. Knox College.

49. Howells, *Selected Letters*, Vol. 3, pp. 201–204.

50. Howells, *Life in Letters*, Vol. 1, p. 402.

51. Knox College.

52. Knox College.

53. Howells, *Life in Letters*, Vol. 1, p. 404.

54. Knox College.

55. Knox College.

56. Knox College.

57. Howells, *Selected Letters*, Vol 3, p. 211.

58. Knox College.

59. Knox College

60. Andrews, *Nook Farm*, p. 54.

61. Howells, *Life in Letters*, Vol. 1, pp. 407–408.

62. Twain and Howells, *Mark Twain–Howells Letters*, Vol. 2, p. 581.

63. Howells, *Life in Letters*, Vol. 1, p. 413.

64. Howells, *Life in Letters*, Vol. 1, p. 416.

65. Howells, *Life in Letters*, Vol. 1, p. 417.

66. Howells, *Selected Letters*, Vol. 3, pp. 236–237.

67. Altgeld, *The Mind and Spirit of John Peter Altgeld*, pp. 65, 95.

68. Avrich, *The Haymarket Tragedy*, p. 424.

69. David, *The History of the Haymarket Affair*, p. 486.
70. Stone, *Clarence Darrow for the Defense*, p. 96.
71. Debs, "The Martyred Apostles of Labor," *New Time*, February 1898; reprinted in Debs, *Life, Writings, and Speeches*, pp. 264–267.
72. Debs, Scrapbook 1, Vol. 4, p. 146; Vol. 7, p. 254; Vol. 9, pp. 31, 79.
73. Howells, *Selected Letters*, Vol. 4, pp. 101, 104.
74. Howells, *Selected Letters*, Vol. 5, p. 330.
75. Hough, *The Quiet Rebel*, p. 38.
76. Howells, *Life in Letters*, Vol. 1, pp. 54–55.
77. Howells, *A Selected Edition*, Vol. 6, p. 4.
78. Brooks, *William Dean Howells*, p. 273.
79. Dreiser, "William Dean Howells," *Success*, April 1898; reprinted in Halfmann, *Interviews with William Dean Howells*, p. 51.
80. Marx and Engels, *Letters to Americans*, p. 146.
81. Cady, *The Realist at War*, p. 81.
82. Howells, *Prefaces to Contemporaries*, pp. 68–72.
83. Howells, *Life in Letters*, Vol. 2, pp. 67–68.
84. Whitlock, *Letters and Journal*, Vol. 1, p. 25.
85. Whitlock, *Forty Years of It*, p. 73.
86. Aptheker, *Annotated Bibliography of the Published Works of W. E. B. Du Bois*, pp. 154, 356 (Items 528, 1035).
87. Howells, *A Selected Edition*, Vol. 20, p. 100.

88. Aaron, *The Unwritten War*, p. 130.

89. Olson, "Socialist and Realist," pp. 56–58.

90. Wagenknecht, *William Dean Howells*, pp. 272–273.

91. Twain and Howells, *Mark Twain-Howells Letters*, Vol. 2, pp. 626–627.

92. Schirmer, *Republic or Empire?* p. 164.

93. Freidel, *The Splendid Little War*, p. 3.

94. Howells, *Life in Letters*, Vol. 2, p. 95.

95. Howells, *Life in Letters*, Vol. 2, p. 361.

96. Howells, *Life in Letters*, Vol. 2, pp. 359–360.

97. Howells, *Selected Letters*, Vol. 6, p. 96.

98. *New York Times*, May 12, 1920.

99. Josephson, *Portrait of the Artist as American*, pp. 164–165.

100. Howells, *Life in Letters*, Vol. 2, pp. 261, 263.

101. Parsons, *The Life of Albert Parsons*, p. 1.

102. Foner, *The Autobiographies of the Haymarket Martyrs*, p. 96.

103. Adelman, *Haymarket Revisited*, p. 50.

Bibliography

Preface

Alger, George W. "The Literature of Exposure." *Atlantic Monthly*, August 1905.

Aptheker, Herbert. *American Negro Slave Revolts*. New York: Columbia University Press, 1943; New York: International Publishers, 1969.

———, ed. *A Documentary History of the Negro People in the United States*. 2 vols. Preface by W. E. B. Du Bois. New York: Citadel Press, 1951, 1964; New York: Carol Publishing Group, 1990.

———. *Afro-American History: The Modern Era*. New York: Citadel Press, 1971.

———. *Annotated Bibliography of the Published Writings of W. E. B. Du Bois*. Millwood, N.Y.: Kraus-Thomson, 1973.

———. *Abolitionism, a Revolutionary Movement*. Boston: Twayne, 1989.

Baker, Ray Stannard. *American Chronicle: The Autobiography of Ray Stannard Baker*. New York: Scribners, 1945.

Baxandall, Rosalyn; Gordon, Linda; and Reverby, Susan, eds. *America's Working Women: A Documentary History, 1600 to the Present.* New York: Random House, 1976.

Berry, Mary Frances, and Blassingame, John W. *Long Memory: The Black Experience in America.* New York: Oxford University Press, 1982.

Bird, Stewart; Georgakas, Dan; and Shaffer, Deborah, eds. *Solidarity Forever: An Oral History of the IWW.* Chicago: Lake View Press, 1985.

Calmer, Alan. *Labor Agitator: The Story of Albert R. Parsons.* Foreword by Lucy E. Parsons. New York: International Publishers, 1937.

Carlson, Peter. *Roughneck: The Life and Times of Big Bill Haywood.* New York: W. W. Norton, 1983.

Conlin, Joseph. *Big Bill Haywood and the Radical Union Movement.* Syracuse, N.Y.: Syracuse University Press, 1969.

Cornell, Frederic. "A History of the Rand School of Social Science, 1906–1956." Ed.D. dissertation, Teachers College, Columbia University, 1976.

Darrow, Clarence. *The Story of My Life.* New York: Grosset and Dunlap, 1932.

———. *Attorney for the Damned.* Edited by Arthur Weinberg. Foreword by William O. Douglas. New York: Simon and Schuster, 1957.

———. *Verdicts Out of Court.* Edited by Arthur Weinberg and Lila S. Weinberg. Chicago: Quadrangle Books, 1963.

De Mille, Anna George. *Henry George, Citizen of the World.* Edited by Don P. Shoemaker. Introduction by Agnes De Mille. Chapel Hill: University of North Carolina Press.

Drinnon, Richard. *Rebel in Paradise: A Biography of Emma Goldman.* Chicago: University of Chicago Press, 1961, 1982.

Du Bois, W. E. B. *The Suppression of the African Slave Trade in the United States of America, 1638–1870.* New York: Longmans, Green, 1896; Millwood, N.Y.: Kraus-Thomson, 1973.

———. *The Souls of Black Folk: Essays and Sketches.* Chicago: A. C. McClurg, 1903; Millwood, N.Y.: Kraus-Thomson, 1975.

———. *John Brown.* Philadelphia: George W. Jacobs, 1909; Millwood, N.Y.: Kraus-Thomson, 1974.

———. *The Gift of Black Folk: The Negroes in the Making of America.* Boston: Stratford, 1924; Millwood, N.Y.: Kraus-Thomson, 1975.

———. *Black Reconstruction: An Essay Toward a History of the Part Which Black Folk Played in the Attempt to Reconstruct Democracy in America, 1860–1880.* New York: Harcourt, Brace, 1935; Millwood, N.Y.: Kraus-Thomson, 1976.

———. *The Autobiography of W. E. B. Du Bois: A Soliloquy on Viewing My Life from the Last Decade of Its First Century.* Edited by Herbert Aptheker. New York: International Publishers, 1968.

———. *The Correspondence of W. E. B. Du Bois.* Edited by Herbert Aptheker. 3 vols. Amherst: University of Massachusetts Press, 1973.

Dubofsky, Melvyn. *We Shall Be All: A History of the Industrial Workers of the World.* Chicago: Quadrangle Books, 1969; Urbana: University of Illinois Press, 1988.

Fetherling, Dale. *Mother Jones, the Miners' Angel: A Portrait.* Carbondale: Southern Illinois University Press, 1974.

Filler, Louis. *The Muckrakers: Crusaders for American Liberalism.* New York: Harcourt, Brace, 1939; University Park: Pennsylvania State University Press, 1976.

———. *Voice of the Democracy: A Critical Biography of David Graham Phillips, Journalist, Novelist, Progressive.* University Park: Pennsylvania State University Press, 1982.

Fine, Nathan. *Labor and Farmer Parties in the United States, 1828–1928.* New York: Rand School of Social Science, 1928; New York: Russell and Russell, 1961.

Fishbein, Leslie. *Rebels in Bohemia: The Radicals of the "Masses," 1911–1917.* Chapel Hill: University of North Carolina Press, 1982.

Flynn, Elizabeth Gurley. *The Rebel Girl: An Autobiography.* New York: International Publishers, 1955; revised edition, 1973.

———. *Words on Fire: The Life and Writing of Elizabeth Gurley Flynn.* Edited by Rosalyn Fraad Baxandall. New Brunswick, N.J.: Rutgers University Press, 1987.

Folsom, Franklin. *Impatient Armies of the Poor: The Story of Collective Action by the Unemployed, 1808–1942.* Niwot: University Press of Colorado, 1991.

Foner, Philip S. *History of the Labor Movement in the United States.* 7 vols. New York: International Publishers, 1947–1965.

Foster, William Z. *Pages from a Worker's Life.* New York: International Publishers, 1939.

Franklin, John Hope. *From Slavery to Freedom: A History of Negro Americans.* New York: Alfred A. Knopf, 1947; revised edition, 1988.

Frost, Richard H. *The Mooney Case.* Stanford, Calif.: Stanford University Press, 1968.

Garrison, Dee. *Mary Heaton Vorse: The Life of an American Insurgent.* Philadelphia: Temple University Press, 1989.

Gentry, Curt. *Frame-Up: The Incredible Case of Tom Mooney and Warren Billings.* New York: W. W. Norton, 1967.

Goldman, Emma. *Living My Life: An Autobiography.* 2 vols. New York: Alfred A. Knopf, 1931; New York: Dover, 1970; Salt Lake City, Utah: G. M. Smith, 1982.

Graham, John, ed. *Yours for the Revolution: The "Appeal to Reason," 1895–1922.* Lincoln: University of Nebraska Press, 1990.

Hapgood, Hutchins. *A Victorian in the Modern World.* New York: Harcourt, Brace, 1939.

Harding, Vincent. *There Is a River: The Black Struggle for Freedom in America.* New York: Harcourt Brace Jovanovich, 1981.

Harris, Leon. *Upton Sinclair, American Rebel.* New York: Thomas Y. Crowell, 1975.

Haywood, William D. ("Big Bill"). *Bill Haywood's Book.* New York: International Publishers, 1929, 1966.

Hill, Joe. *The Letters of Joe Hill.* Edited by Philip S. Foner. New York: Oak Publications, 1965.

Horton, Russell M. *Lincoln Steffens.* New York: Twayne, 1974.

Jones, Jacqueline. *Labor of Love, Labor of Sorrow: Black Women, Work, and the Family from Slavery to the Present.* New York: Basic Books, 1985.

Jones, Mary ("Mother"). *The Autobiography of Mother Jones.* Edited by Mary Field Parton. Foreword by Clarence Darrow. Chicago: Charles H. Kerr, for the Illinois Labor History Society, 1925, 1974.

———. *The Correspondence of Mother Jones.* Edited by Edward M. Steel. Pittsburgh: University of Pittsburgh Press, 1985.

Lyons, Peter. *Success Story: The Life and Times of S. S. McClure.* New York: Scribners, 1963.

Mandel, Bernard. *Labor, Free and Slave: Workingmen and the Anti-Slavery Movement in the United States.* New York: Associated Authors, 1955.

Marable, Manning. *W. E. B. Du Bois, Black Radical Democrat.* Boston: Twayne, 1986.

Marcaccio, Michael D. *The Hapgoods, Three Earnest Brothers.* Charlottesville: University Press of Virginia, 1977.

McGovern, George S., and Guttridge, Leonard F. *The Great Colorado Coalfield War.* Boston: Houghton Mifflin, 1972.

Meltzer, Milton. *Bread and Roses: The Struggle of American Labor, 1865–1915.* New York: Alfred A. Knopf, 1967; New York: New American Library, 1977.

Morlan, Robert L. *Political Prairie Fire: The Non-Partisan League, 1915–1922.* Minneapolis: University of Minnesota Press, 1955.

Nearing, Scott. *The Making of a Radical: A Political Autobiography.* New York: Harper and Row, 1972.

———. *A Scott Nearing Reader: The Good Life in Bad Times.* Edited by Steve Sherman. Foreword by Helen K. Nearing. Metuchen, N.J.: Scarecrow Press, 1989.

Noble, Jeanne. *Beautiful, Also, Are the Souls of My Black Sisters: A History of the Black Woman in America.* Englewood Cliffs, N.J.: Prentice-Hall, 1978.

O'Neill, William L., ed. *Echoes of Revolt: The "Masses," 1911–1917.* Chicago: Quadrangle Books, 1966.

———. *Feminism in America: A History.* New Brunswick, N.J.: Transaction Books, 1989.

Quarles, Benjamin. *The Negro in the Making of America.* New York: Collier Books, 1964; revised edition, 1987.

Rampersad, Arnold. *The Art and Imagination of W. E. B. Du Bois.* Cambridge, Mass.: Harvard University Press, 1976; New York: Schocken Books, 1990.

Redding, J. Saunders. *Lonesome Road: The Story of the Negro's Part in America.* Garden City, N.Y.: Doubleday, 1958.

Reed, John. *Insurgent Mexico.* New York: D. Appleton, 1914; New York: Simon and Schuster, 1969.

———. *The War in Eastern Europe.* Illustrated by Boardman Robinson. New York: Scribners, 1916.

———. *Ten Days That Shook the World.* Introduction by V. I. Lenin. New York: International Publishers, 1919, 1967.

———. *The Education of John Reed: Selected Writings.* Edited by John Stuart. New York: International Publishers, 1955.

———. *John Reed for the "Masses."* Edited by John C. Wilson. Jefferson, N.C.: McFarland, 1987.

Rosenstone, Robert A. *Romantic Revolutionary: A Biography of John Reed.* New York: Alfred A. Knopf, 1975.

Schluter, Herman. *Lincoln, Labor, and Slavery: A Chapter from the Social History of America.* New York: Socialist Literature Company, 1913; New York: Russell and Russell, 1965.

Schwantes, Carlos A. *Coxey's Army: An American Odyssey.* Lincoln: University of Nebraska Press, 1985.

Schwartz, Rachel Cutler. "The Rand School of Social Science, 1906–1924: A Study of Worker Education in the Socialist Era." Ed.D. dissertation, State University of New York at Buffalo, 1984.

Scott, Clifford H. *Lester F. Ward.* Boston: Twayne, 1976.

Sinclair, Upton. *The Jungle.* New York: Jungle Publishing Company, 1906; Memphis, Tenn.: St. Luke's Press, 1988.

———. *The Cry for Justice: An Anthology of the Literature of Social Protest.* Introduction by Jack London. Philadelphia: John C. Winston, 1915; revised edition, New York: Lyle Stuart, 1964.

———. *The Brass Check: A Study of American Journalism.* Pasadena, Calif.: published by the author, 1920.

———. *The Goose-Step: A Study of American Education.* Pasadena, Calif.: published by the author; New York: AMS Press, 1970.

———. *My Lifetime in Letters.* Columbia: University of Missouri Press, 1960.

———. *The Autobiography of Upton Sinclair.* New York: Harcourt, Brace, 1962.

Smith, Gibbs M. *Joe Hill.* Salt Lake City: University of Utah Press, 1969.

Steffens, Lincoln. *The Autobiography of Lincoln Steffens.* 2 vols. New York: Harcourt, Brace, 1931, 1958.

———. *The Letters of Lincoln Steffens.* Edited by Ella Winter and Granville Hicks. 2 vols. New York: Harcourt, Brace, 1938.

Stone, Irving. *Clarence Darrow for the Defense: A Biography.* Garden City, N.Y.: Doubleday, Doran, 1941; New York: New American Library, 1971.

Tarbell, Ida M. *All in the Day's Work: An Autobiography.* New York: Macmillan, 1939.

Tierney, Kevin. *Darrow: A Biography.* New York: Thomas Y. Crowell, 1979.

Vorse, Mary Heaton. *A Footnote to Folly: An Autobiography.* New York: Farrar and Rinehart, 1935; New York: Arno Press, 1980.

———. *Rebel Pen: The Writings of Mary Heaton Vorse.* Edited by Dee Garrison. New York: Monthly Review Press, 1985.

Wertheimer, Barbara M. *We Were There: The Story of Working Women in America.* New York: Pantheon Books, 1977.

Whitfield, Stephen J. *Scott Nearing, Apostle of American Radicalism.* New York: Columbia University Press, 1974.

Wolff, Leon. *Lockout: The Story of the Homestead Strike of 1892.* New York: Harper and Row, 1965.

Zinn, Howard. *The Politics of History.* Boston: Beacon Press, 1970; revised edition, Urbana: University of Illinois Press, 1990.

———. *A People's History of the United States.* New York: Harper and Row, 1980.

Zipser, Arthur. *Working-Class Giant: The Life of William Z. Foster.* New York: International Publishers, 1981.

John Swinton, Crusading Editor

Allen, Gay Wilson. *The Solitary Singer: A Critical Biography of Walt Whitman.* New York: Macmillan, 1955.

Bartlett, Irving R. *Wendell and Ann Phillips: The Community of Reform, 1840–1880.* New York: W. W. Norton, 1979.

Berger, Meyer. *The Story of the "New York Times," 1851–1951.* New York: Simon and Schuster, 1951.

Boyer, Richard O. *The Legend of John Brown: A Biography and a History.* New York: Alfred A. Knopf, 1973.

Calmer, Alan. *Labor Agitator: The Story of Albert R. Parsons.* Foreword by Lucy E. Parsons. New York: International Publishers, 1937.

Carpenter, George Rice. *Walt Whitman.* New York: Macmillan, 1924.

Debs, Eugene V. *Life, Writings, and Speeches.* Girard, Kans.: Appeal to Reason, 1908.

———. "John Swinton, Radical Editor and Leader." *Pearson's Magazine*, February 1918. Reprinted in *Pastels of Men.* New York: Pearson's Library, 1919; Berkeley Heights, N.J.: Oriole Press, 1939.

———. *Walls and Bars.* Chicago: Socialist Party, 1927; Chicago: Charles H. Kerr, 1973.

———. *Letters of Eugene V. Debs.* Edited by J. Robert Constantine. 3 vols. Urbana: University of Illinois Press, 1990.

Destler, Chester M. *American Radicalism, 1865–1901.* New London: Connecticut College Press, 1946.

———. *Henry Demarest Lloyd and the Empire of Reform.* Philadelphia: University of Pennsylvania Press, 1963.

Du Bois, W. E. B. *John Brown.* Philadelphia: George W. Jacobs, 1909; Millwood, N.Y.: Kraus-Thomson, 1974.

Eble, Kenneth E. *Old Clemens and W.D.H.: The Story of a Remarkable Friendship.* Baton Rouge: University of Louisiana Press, 1985.

Edwards, Stewart. *The Paris Commune, 1871.* London: Eyre and Spottiswoode, 1971.

Ely, Richard T. *Ground Under Our Feet: An Autobiography.* New York: Macmillan, 1938.

Fine, Nathan. *Labor and Farmer Parties in the United States, 1818–1928.* New York: Rand School of Social Science, 1928; New York: Russell and Russell, 1961.

Folsom, Franklin. *Impatient Armies of the Poor: The Story of Collective Action by the Unemployed, 1808–1942.* Niwot: University Press of Colorado, 1991.

Foner, Philip S. *History of the Labor Movement in the United States.* 7 vols. New York: International Publishers, 1947–1965.

———. *Mark Twain, Social Critic.* New York: International Publishers, 1958.

———, ed. *When Karl Marx Died: Comments in 1883.* New York: International Publishers, 1973.

———. "Protests in the United States Against Bismarck's Anti-Socialist Law." *International Review of Social History*, Vol. 21, Part 1 (1976).

———. *The Great Labor Upheaval of 1877.* New York: Monad Press, 1977.

———. *Women and the American Labor Movement.* 2 vols. New York: Free Press, 1980.

Ghent, W. J. "John Swinton." In *Dictionary of American Biography.* Vol. 18. Edited by Dumas Malone. New York: Scribners, 1936.

Ginger, Ray. *The Bending Cross: A Biography of Eugene V. Debs.* New Brunswick, N.J.: Rutgers University Press, 1949; New York: Russell and Russell, 1969.

Gutman, Herbert G. "The Tompkins Square 'Riot' in New York City of January 13, 1874: A Reexamination of Its Causes and Its Effects." *Labor History*, Vol. 6 (Winter 1965).

Harris, Leon. *Upton Sinclair, American Rebel.* New York: Thomas Y. Crowell, 1975.

Healey, Edna. *Wives of Fame: Mary Livingstone, Jenny Marx, and Emma Darwin.* London: Sidgwick and Jackson, 1986.

Holloway, Emory. *Whitman: An Interpretation in Narrative.* New York: Alfred A. Knopf, 1926.

Hough, Robert L. *The Quiet Rebel: William Dean Howells as Social Commentator.* Lincoln: University of Nebraska Press, 1959.

James, Edward T. "John W. Hayes." In *Dictionary of American Biography.* Supp. 3. Edited by Edward T. James. New York: Scribners, 1973.

Jellinek, Frank. *The Paris Commune of 1871.* New York: Oxford University Press, 1937.

Kaplan, Justin. *Mr. Clemens and Mark Twain: A Biography.* New York: Simon and Schuster, 1966.

———. *Walt Whitman: A Life.* New York: Simon and Schuster, 1980.

Kapp, Yvonne. *Eleanor Marx.* 2 vols. New York: Pantheon Books, 1977.

Karsner, David. *Horace Traubel: His Life and Work.* New York: E. Arens, 1919.

Kaufman, Stuart B. *Samuel Gompers and the Origins of the American Federation of Labor, 1848–1896.* Westport, Conn.: Greenwood Press, 1973.

Levine, Susan. "Their Own Sphere: Women's Work, the Knights of Labor, and the Transformation of the Carpet Trade, 1870–1890." Ph.D. dissertation, City University of New York, 1979.

Lidtke, Vernon *The Alternative Culture: Socialist Labor in Imperial Germany.* New York: Oxford University Press, 1985.

Lloyd, Caro. *Henry Demarest Lloyd: A Biography, 1847–1903.* 2 vols. New York: Putnam, 1912.

Mandel, Bernard. *Samuel Gompers: A Biography.* Yellow Springs, Ohio: Antioch Press, 1963.

Marx, Eleanor, and Aveling, Edward. *The Working-Class Movement in America.* London: Swan, Sonnenschein, 1890; New York: Arno Press, 1969.

Marx, Eleanor; Lafargue, Laura Marx; and Longuet, Jenny Marx. *The Daughters of Karl Marx: Family Correspondence, 1866–1898.* Translated by Faith Evans. Notes and commentary by Olga Meier. Introduction by Sheila Rowbotham. New York: Harcourt, Brace, 1982.

Marx, Karl, and Engels, Frederick. *Letters to Americans, 1848–1895.* Translated by Leonard E. Mins. Edited by Alexander Trachtenberg. New York: International Publishers, 1953.

Maverick, Augustus. *Henry J. Raymond and the New York Press.* Hartford: A. S. Hale, 1870; New York: Arno Press, 1970.

Mehring, Franz. *Karl Marx.* Translated by Edward Fitzgerald. Edited by Ruth and Heinz Norden. New York: Covici, Friede, 1935.

Meltzer, Milton. *Mark Twain Himself: A Pictorial Biography.* New York: Thomas Y. Crowell, 1960.

———. *Bread and Roses: The Struggle of American Labor, 1865–1915.* New York: Alfred A. Knopf, 1967; New York: New American Library, 1977.

O'Brien, Frank M. *The Story of the "Sun," 1833–1928.* New York: D. Appleton, 1928.

Perlman, Selig. *A History of Trade Unionism in the United States.* New York: Macmillan, 1922; New York: Augustus M. Kelley, 1950.

———. "John Swinton." In *Encyclopedia of the Social Sciences*, edited by Edwin R. A. Seligman and Alvin Johnson. Vol. 14. New York: Macmillan, 1934.

Phillips, Wendell. *Wendell Phillips on Civil Rights and Freedom.* Edited by Louis Filler. New York: Hill and Wang, 1965.

Ross, Marc. "John Swinton, Journalist and Reformer: The Active Years, 1857–1887." Ph.D. dissertation, New York University, 1969.

Salvatore, Nick. *Eugene V. Debs, Citizen and Socialist.* Urbana: University of Illinois Press, 1982.

Sherwin, Oscar. *Prophet of Liberty: The Life and Times of Wendell Phillips.* New York: Bookman Associates, 1958.

Sinclair, Upton. *The Jungle.* New York: Jungle Publishing Company, 1906; Memphis, Tenn.: St. Luke's Press, 1988.

———. *The Cry for Justice: An Anthology of the Literature of Social Protest.* Introduction by Jack London. Philadelphia: John C. Winston, 1915; revised edition, New York: Lyle Stuart, 1964.

———. *The Brass Check: A Study of American Journalism.* Pasadena, Calif.: published by the author, 1920.

———. *The Goose-Step: A Study of American Education.* Pasadena, Calif.: published by the author; New York: AMS Press, 1970.

———. *My Lifetime in Letters.* Columbia: University of Missouri Press, 1960.

———. *The Autobiography of Upton Sinclair.* New York: Harcourt, Brace, 1962.

Sorge, Friedrich A. *The Labor Movement in the United States: A History of the American Working Class from Colonial Times to 1890.* Translated by Brewster Chamberlin and Angela Chamberlin. Edited by Philip S. Foner and Brewster Chamberlin. Westport, Conn.: Greenwood Press, 1977.

———. *The Labor Movement in the United States: A History of the American Working Class from 1890 to 1896*. Translated by Kai Schoenhals. New York: Greenwood Press, 1987.

Spaulding, Thomas M. "William Swinton." In *Dictionary of American Biography*. Vol. 18. Edited by Dumas Malone. New York: Scribners, 1936.

Stepanchev, Stephen. "Whitman in Russia." In *Walt Whitman Abroad*, edited by Gay Wilson Allen. Syracuse, N.Y.: Syracuse University Press, 1955.

Stewart, James B. *Wendell Phillips, Liberty's Hero*. Baton Rouge: Louisiana State University Press, 1986.

Swinton, John. *The New Issue: The Chinese-American Question*. New York: American News Company, 1870.

———. *The Tompkins Square Outrage: Appeal of John Swinton. Address to the New York State Legislature Through the Committee on Grievances, Delivered to the Assembly Chamber at Albany, March 25, 1874*. Albany: n.p., 1874.

———. *John Swinton's Travels: Current Views and Notes of Forty Days in France and England*. New York: C. W. Carleton, 1880.

———. *Old Osawatomie Brown: Speech on the Twenty-Second Anniversary of John Brown's Death. Delivered at Turnverein Hall, New York, December 1, 1881*. New York: n.p., 1881.

———. *John Swinton's Paper*, 1883–1887. Tamiment Library, New York University.

———. *John Swinton's Address Before the American Federation of Labor Convention at Philadelphia, 1892*. New York: American Federation of Labor, 1893.

———. *Striking for Life: Labor's Side of the Labor Question.* New York: American Manufacturing and Publishing Company, 1894; Westport, Conn.: Greenwood Press, 1970. Reprinted as *A Momentous Question: The Respective Attitudes of Labor and Capital.* Philadelphia: A. R. Keller, 1895; New York: Arno Press, 1969; New York: Burt Franklin, 1971.

Traubel, Horace. *Chants Communal.* Boston: Small, Maynard, 1904.

———. *With Walt Whitman in Camden.* 6 vols. Vol. 1, Boston: Small, Maynard, 1906; Vol. 2, New York: D. Appleton, 1908; Vol. 3, New York: Mitchell Kennerley, 1914; Vol. 4, Philadelphia: University of Pennsylvania Press, 1953; Vols. 5, 6, Carbondale: Southern Illinois University Press, 1964, 1982.

———. *Optimos.* New York: B. W. Huebsch, 1910.

Tsuzuki, Chushichi. *The Life of Eleanor Marx, 1855–1898: A Socialist Tragedy.* Oxford: Clarendon Press, 1967.

Twain, Mark, and Howells, William Dean. *Mark Twain–Howells Letters.* Edited by Henry Nash Smith and William M. Gibson. 2 vols. Cambridge, Mass.: Belknap Press of Harvard University Press, 1960.

Walling, William English. *Whitman and Traubel.* New York: Albert and Charles Boni, 1916.

Waters, Robert. *Career and Conversation of John Swinton, Journalist, Orator, and Economist.* Chicago: Charles H. Kerr, 1902.

Whitman, Walt. *The Correspondence of Walt Whitman.* 6 vols. Edited by Edwin Haviland Miller. New York: New York University Press, 1961–1977.

———. *Leaves of Grass.* Edited by Harold W. Blodgett and Sculley Bradley. New York: W. W. Norton, 1973.

———. *The Poetry and Prose of Walt Whitman.* Edited by Justin Kaplan. New York: Library of America, 1982.

———. *Notebooks and Unpublished Prose Manuscripts.* Edited by Edward F. Grier. New York: New York University Press, 1984.

Charles P. Steinmetz, Scientist and Socialist

Anikeyev, V. V., and Solovyov, A. A., eds. *Lenin Through the Eyes of the World.* Translated by K. M. Cook. Moscow: Progress Publishers, 1969.

Annual Report, 1923. Schenectady: General Electric Company, December 31, 1923.

Annual Reports of the Commissioner of Patents. Washington, D.C.: U.S. Government Printing Office, 1900–1923.

Bailey, Thomas A., and Ryan, Paul B. *The "Lusitania" Disaster: An Episode in Modern Warfare and Diplomacy.* New York: Free Press, 1975.

Bibber, Harold W. *Charles Proteus Steinmetz.* Union Worthies, No. 20. Schenectady: Union College, 1965.

Bloor, Ella Reeve. *We Are Many: An Autobiography.* Introduction by Elizabeth Gurley Flynn. New York: International Publishers, 1940.

Broderick, John F. *Steinmetz and His Discoverer.* Schenectady: Robson and Adee, 1924.

———. *Forty Years with General Electric.* Albany: Fort Orange Press, 1928.

Caldecott, Ernest, and Alger, Philip L., eds. *Steinmetz the Philosopher.* Schenectady: Mohawk, 1966.

Carlson, Peter. *Roughneck: The Life and Times of Big Bill Haywood.* New York: W. W. Norton, 1983.

Claessens, August. *Didn't We Have Fun! Stories Out of a Long, Fruitful, and Merry Life.* New York: Rand School Press, 1953.

Clark, Ronald W. *Lenin.* New York: Harper and Row, 1988.

Coleman, McAlister. "Charles P. Steinmetz." In *Pioneers of Freedom.* Introduction by Norman Thomas. New York: Vanguard Press, 1929.

Conlin, Joseph. *Big Bill Haywood and the Radical Union Movement.* Syracuse, N.Y.: Syracuse University Press, 1969.

Debs, Eugene V. *Life, Writings, and Speeches.* Girard, Kans.: Appeal to Reason, 1908.

———. *Walls and Bars.* Chicago: Socialist Party, 1927; Chicago: Charles H. Kerr, 1973.

———. *Letters of Eugene V. Debs.* Edited by J. Robert Constantine. 3 vols. Urbana: University of Illinois Press, 1990.

Dos Passos, John. *The Forty-Second Parallel* (Part 1 of *U.S.A.*). New York: Modern Library, 1937; Boston: Houghton Mifflin, 1963.

Du Bois, W. E. B. "A Field for Socialists." *New Review,* January 1913.

———. "Socialism and the Negro Problem." *New Review,* February 1913.

———. "Another Study in Black." *New Review,* July 1914.

———. *The Autobiography of W. E. B. Du Bois: A Soliloquy on Viewing My Life from the Last Decade of Its First Century.* Edited by Herbert Aptheker. New York: International Publishers, 1968.

———. *The Correspondence of W. E. B. Du Bois.* Edited by Herbert Aptheker. 3 vols. Amherst: University of Massachusetts Press, 1973.

Egbert, Donald Drew, and Persons, Stow, eds. *Socialism and American Life.* 2 vols. Princeton, N.J.: Princeton University Press, 1952.

Flynn, Elizabeth Gurley. *The Rebel Girl: An Autobiography.* New York: International Publishers, 1955; revised edition, 1973.

———. *Words on Fire: The Life and Writing of Elizabeth Gurley Flynn.* Edited by Rosalyn Fraad Baxandall. New Brunswick, N.J.: Rutgers University Press, 1987.

Forcey, Charles. *The Crossroads of Liberalism: Croly, Weyl, Lippmann, and the Progressive Era.* New York: Oxford University Press, 1961.

Foster, William Z. *Pages from a Worker's Life.* New York: International Publishers, 1939.

Freeman, Lucy; La Follette, Sherry; and Zabriskie, George. *Belle: The Biography of Belle Case La Follette.* New York: Beaufort Books, 1985.

Garrison, Dee. *Mary Heaton Vorse: The Life of an American Insurgent.* Philadelphia: Temple University Press, 1989.

Ginger, Ray. *The Bending Cross: A Biography of Eugene Victor Debs.* New Brunswick, N.J.: Rutgers University Press, 1949; New York: Russell and Russell, 1969.

Hammond, John Winthrop. *Charles Proteus Steinmetz: A Biography.* New York: Century, 1924.

Harris, Lement. *Harold M. Ware, Agricultural Pioneer, USA and USSR.* New York: American Institute for Marxist Studies, 1981.

Harris, Leon. *Upton Sinclair, American Rebel.* New York: Thomas Y. Crowell, 1975.

Hart, Larry. *Schenectady and the Golden Era, 1890–1930.* Scotia, N.Y.: Old Dorp Books, 1974.

———. *Steinmetz in Schenectady: A Picture Story of Three Memorable Decades.* Scotia, N.Y.: Old Dorp Books, 1978.

Heller, A. A. *The Industrial Revival in Soviet Russia.* Introduction by Charles P. Steinmetz. New York: Thomas Seltzer, 1922.

Hendrickson, K. E., Jr. "George R. Lunn and the Socialist Era in Schenectady, 1909–1916." *Proceedings of the New York State Historical Association*, Vol. 64 (1916).

Hillquit, Morris. *Loose Leaves from a Busy Life.* New York: Macmillan, 1934.

Hoeling, Adolph A., and Hoeling, Mary. *The Last Voyage of the "Lusitania."* New York: Henry Holt, 1956.

Horton, Russell M. *Lincoln Steffens.* New York: Twayne, 1974.

Johnson, Walter, ed. *Selected Letters of William Allen White.* New York: Henry Holt, 1947.

Keller, Helen. *Helen Keller: Her Socialist Years.* Edited by Philip S. Foner. New York: International Publishers, 1967.

La Follette, Belle Case, and La Follette, Fola. *La Follette.* 2 vols. New York: Macmillan, 1953.

La Follette, Robert M. *La Follette's Autobiography: A Personal Narrative of Political Experiences.* Madison: published by the author, 1913; Madison: University of Wisconsin Press, 1968.

Lamont, Corliss. *Albert Rhys Williams: In Memoriam.* New York: Horizon Press, 1962.

Lamson, Peggy. *Roger Baldwin, Founder of the American Civil Liberties Union: A Portrait.* Boston: Houghton Mifflin, 1976.

Lazarus, Louis. "References on Steinmetz in the Socialist Literature." Tamiment Library, New York University.

Lenin, V. I. *Collected Works.* Vols. 31, 35, 45. Moscow: Progress Publishers, 1966, 1970.

———. *Lenin on the United States: Selected Writings.* New York: International Publishers, 1970.

Leonard, Jonathan N. *Loki: The Life of Charles Proteus Steinmetz.* Garden City, N.Y.: Doubleday, Doran, 1929.

Levin, Dan. *Stormy Petrel: The Life and Work of Maxim Gorky.* New York: Appleton-Century, 1965.

Lidtke, Vernon *The Alternative Culture: Socialist Labor in Imperial Germany.* New York: Oxford University Press, 1985.

Lippmann, Walter. "Harvard in Politics: A Problem in Imperceptibles." *Harvard Monthly*, Vol. 49 (December 1909).

———. *A Preface to Politics.* New York: Mitchell Kennerley, 1913; New York: Macmillan, 1933.

Marable, Manning. *W. E. B. Du Bois, Black Radical Democrat.* Boston: Twayne, 1986.

Mason, Daniel; Smith, Jessica; and Laibman, David, eds. *Lenin's Impact on the United States.* New York: New World Review, 1970.

Matles, James J., and Higgins, James. *Them and Us: Struggles of a Rank-and-File Union.* Englewood Cliffs, N.J.: Prentice-Hall, 1974.

Maurer, James H. *It Can Be Done: The Autobiography of James H. Maurer.* New York: Rand School Press, 1938.

Morray, J. P. *Project Kuzbas: American Workers in Siberia, 1921–1926.* New York: International Publishers, 1983.

Myers, Gustavus. *History of the Great American Fortunes.* 3 vols. Chicago: Charles H. Kerr, 1907–1910; New York: Modern Library, 1936.

Pratt, Norma Fain. *Morris Hillquit: A Political History of an American Jewish Socialist.* Westport, Conn.: Greenwood Press, 1979.

Rampersad, Arnold. *The Art and Imagination of W. E. B. Du Bois.* Cambridge, Mass.: Harvard University Press, 1976; New York: Schocken Books, 1990.

Salvatore, Nick. *Eugene V. Debs, Citizen and Socialist.* Urbana: University of Illinois Press, 1982.

Simpson, Colin. *The "Lusitania."* Boston: Little, Brown, 1973.

Sinclair, Upton. *My Lifetime in Letters.* Columbia: University of Missouri Press, 1960.

———. *The Autobiography of Upton Sinclair.* New York: Harcourt, Brace, 1962.

State of New York. *Proceedings of the Judiciary Committee of the Assembly.* "In the Matter of the Investigation by the Assembly of the State of New York as to the Qualifications of Louis Waldman, August Claessens, Samuel Orr, and Charles Solomon to Retain Their Seats in Said Body." 3 vols. Albany: J. B. Lyon, 1920.

Steel, Ronald. *Walter Lippmann and the American Century.* Boston: Little, Brown, 1980.

Steffens, Lincoln. *The Autobiography of Lincoln Steffens.* 2 vols. New York: Harcourt, Brace, 1931, 1958.

———. *The Letters of Lincoln Steffens.* Edited by Ella Winter and Granville Hicks. 2 vols. New York: Harcourt, Brace, 1938.

Steinmetz, Charles P. *America and the New Epoch.* New York: Harper and Brothers, 1916.

Vorse, Mary Heaton. *A Footnote to Folly: An Autobiography.* New York: Farrar and Rinehart, 1935; New York: Arno Press, 1980.

———. *Rebel Pen: The Writings of Mary Heaton Vorse.* Edited by Dee Garrison. New York: Monthly Review Press, 1985.

Weinstein, James. *The Decline of Socialism in America, 1912–1925.* New Brunswick, N.J.: Rutgers University Press, 1967; revised edition, 1984.

Zipser, Arthur. *Working-Class Giant: The Life of William Z. Foster.* New York: International Publishers, 1981.

Zipser, Arthur, and Zipser, Pearl. *Fire and Grace: The Life of Rose Pastor Stokes.* Athens: University of Georgia Press, 1989.

William Dean Howells and the Haymarket Era

Aaron, Daniel. *Men of Good Hope: A Story of American Progressives.* New York: Oxford University Press, 1951, 1961.

______. *The Unwritten War: American Writers and the Civil War.* New York: Alfred A. Knopf, 1973; Madison: University of Wisconsin Press, 1987.

Abrams, Irving. *Haymarket Heritage: The Memoirs of Irving Abrams.* Edited by David R. Roediger and Phyllis Boanes. Chicago: Charles H. Kerr, for the Illinois Labor History Society, 1989.

Addams, Jane. *Twenty Years at Hull House.* New York: Macmillan, 1910; Urbana: University of Illinois Press, 1990.

______. *The Second Twenty Years at Hull House.* New York: Macmillan, 1930.

______. "Henry Demarest Lloyd." In *The Excellent Becomes the Permanent.* New York: Macmillan, 1932; Freeport, N.Y.: Books for Libraries Press, 1970.

______. *The Social Thought of Jane Addams.* Edited by Christopher Lasch. New York: Macmillan, 1965; New York: Irvington, 1982.

Adelman, William J. *Haymarket Revisited: A Tour Guide to Labor-History Sites and Ethnic Neighborhoods Connected with the Haymarket Affair.* Chicago: Charles H. Kerr, for the Illinois Labor History Society, 1976.

______. *Touring Pullman: A Study in Company Paternalism.* Chicago: Charles H. Kerr, for the Illinois Labor History Society, 1977.

———. *Pilsen and the West Side: A Tour Guide to Ethnic Neighborhoods, Architecture, Restaurants, Wall Murals, and Labor History, with Special Emphasis on Events Connected with the Great Upheaval of 1877.* Chicago: Charles H. Kerr, for the Illinois Labor History Society, 1983.

Altgeld, John Peter. *The Mind and Spirit of John Peter Altgeld: Selected Writings and Addresses.* Edited by Henry A. Christman. Urbana: University of Illinois Press, 1960.

Anderson, David D. *Brand Whitlock.* New York: Twayne, 1968.

Andrews, Kenneth. *Nook Farm: Mark Twain's Hartford Circle.* Cambridge, Mass.: Harvard University Press, 1950.

Andrews, William L. "William Dean Howells and Charles W. Chesnutt: Criticism and Race Fiction in the Age of Booker T. Washington." *American Literature*, Vol. 48 (1976).

Aptheker, Herbert. *Annotated Bibliography of the Published Writings of W. E. B. Du Bois.* Millwood, N.Y.: Kraus-Thomson, 1973.

Arms, George. "Further Inquiry into Howells's Socialism." *Science and Society*, Vol. 3 (1939).

———. "The Literary Background of Howells's Social Criticism." *American Literature*, Vol. 17 (May 1945).

Ashbaugh, Carolyn. *Lucy Parsons, American Revolutionary.* Chicago: Charles H. Kerr, for the Illinois Labor History Society, 1976.

Avrich, Paul. *The Haymarket Tragedy.* Princeton, N.J.: Princeton University Press, 1984.

———. *Anarchist Portraits.* Princeton, N.J.: Princeton University Press, 1988.

———. *Sacco and Vanzetti: The Anarchist Background.* Princeton, N.J.: Princeton University Press, 1991.

Barnard, Harry. *Eagle Forgotten: The Life of John Peter Altgeld.* New York: Duell, Sloan, and Pearce, 1938; Indianapolis: Bobbs-Merrill, 1962.

Bass, Altha Leah. "The Social Consciousness of William Dean Howells." *New Republic*, August 13, 1921.

Becker, George J. "William Dean Howells: The Awakening of Conscience." *College English*, April 1958.

Bellamy, Edward. *Looking Backward, 2000–1887.* Boston: Houghton, Mifflin, 1887; Cambridge, Mass.: Belknap Press of Harvard University Press, 1967.

Bennett, George N. *William Dean Howells: The Development of a Novelist.* Norman: University of Oklahoma Press, 1959.

———. *The Realism of William Dean Howells, 1889–1920.* Nashville, Tenn.: Vanderbilt University Press, 1973.

Besant, Annie. *A Selection of the Social and Political Pamphlets of Annie Besant.* Edited by John Saville. New York: Augustus M. Kelley, 1970.

Borus, Daniel H. *Writing Realism: Howells, James, and Norris in the Mass Market.* Chapel Hill: University of North Carolina Press, 1989.

Bowman, Sylvia E. *The Year 2000: A Critical Biography of Edward Bellamy.* New York: Bookman Associates, 1958.

Brawley, Benjamin. *Paul Laurence Dunbar, Poet of His People.* Chapel Hill: University of North Carolina Press, 1936.

Brooks, Van Wyck. *Howells: His Life and World.* New York: E. P. Dutton, 1959.

Brown, Ford Madox. *The Diary of Ford Madox Brown.* Edited by Virginia Surtees. New Haven, Conn.: Yale University Press, 1981.

Browne, Waldo R. *Altgeld of Illinois: A Record of His Life and Work.* New York: B. W. Huebsch, 1924.

Buchanan, Joseph R. *The Story of a Labor Agitator.* New York: Outlook, 1903; Westport, Conn.: Greenwood Press, 1970; Freeport, N.Y.: Books for Universities Press, 1971.

Budd, Louis J. "William Dean Howells's Debt to Tolstoy." *American Slavic and East European Review*, Vol. 9 (December 1950).

———. "Twain, Howells, and the Boston Nihilists." *New England Quarterly*, Vol. 32 (September 1959).

Cady, Edwin H. "The Gentleman as Socialist: William Dean Howells." In *The Gentleman in America: A Literary Study in American Culture.* Syracuse, N.Y.: Syracuse University Press, 1949.

———. *The Road to Realism: The Early Years of William Dean Howells, 1837–1885.* Syracuse, N.Y.: Syracuse University Press, 1956.

———. *The Realist at War: The Mature Years of William Dean Howells, 1885–1920.* Syracuse, N.Y.: Syracuse University Press, 1958.

———. *Young Howells and John Brown: Episodes in a Radical Education.* Columbus: Ohio State University Press, 1985.

Cahan, Abraham. *The Education of Abraham Cahan.* Translated by Leon Stein, Abraham P. Conan, and Lynn Davison. Philadelphia: Jewish Publication Society of America, 1969.

Calmer, Alan. *Labor Agitator: The Story of Albert R. Parsons.* Foreword by Lucy E. Parsons. New York: International Publishers, 1937.

Carlson, Peter. *Roughneck: The Life and Times of Big Bill Haywood.* New York: W. W. Norton, 1983.

Carter, Everett. "The Haymarket Affair in Literature." *American Quarterly,* Vol. 2, No. 3 (Fall 1950).

Chalmers, W. Ellison. "Laurence Gronlund." In *Dictionary of American Biography.* Vol. 8. Edited by Dumas Malone. New York: Scribners, 1936.

Conlin, Joseph. *Big Bill Haywood and the Radical Union Movement.* Syracuse, N.Y.: Syracuse University Press, 1969.

Crunden, Robert M. *A Hero in Spite of Himself: Brand Whitlock in Art, Politics, and War.* New York: Alfred A. Knopf, 1969.

Darrow, Clarence. *The Story of My Life.* New York: Grosset and Dunlap, 1932.

———. *Attorney for the Damned.* Edited by Arthur Weinberg. Foreword by William O. Douglas. New York: Simon and Schuster, 1957.

———. *Verdicts Out of Court.* Edited by Arthur Weinberg and Lila S. Weinberg. Chicago: Quadrangle Books, 1963.

David, Henry. *The History of the Haymarket Affair: A Study in the American Social-Revolutionary and Labor Movements.* New York: Farrar and Rinehart, 1936; New York: Russell and Russell, 1958 (new introduction); New York: Collier Books, 1963 (footnotes deleted).

Debs, Eugene V. Scrapbooks. Tamiment Library, New York University.

———. *Life, Writings, and Speeches.* Girard, Kans.: Appeal to Reason, 1908.

———. *Walls and Bars.* Chicago: Socialist Party, 1927; Chicago: Charles H. Kerr, 1973.

———. *Letters.* Edited by J. Robert Constantine. Urbana: University of Illinois Press, 1990.

De Mille, Anna George. *Henry George, Citizen of the World.* Edited by Don P. Shoemaker. Introduction by Agnes De Mille. Chapel Hill: University of North Carolina Press, 1950.

Destler, Chester M. *American Radicalism, 1865–1901: Essays and Documents.* New London: Connecticut College Press, 1946; Chicago: Quadrangle Books, 1966.

———. *Henry Demarest Lloyd and the Empire of Reform.* Philadelphia: University of Pennsylvania Press, 1963.

Dombrowski, James. *The Early Years of Christian Socialism.* New York: Columbia University Press, 1936; New York: Octagon Books, 1966 .

Dorfman, Joseph. *Thorstein Veblen and His America.* New York: Viking Press, 1934; New York: Augustus M. Kelley, 1961.

Drinnon, Richard. *Rebel in Paradise: A Biography of Emma Goldman.* Chicago: University of Chicago Press, 1961, 1982.

Du Bois, W. E. B. *The Autobiography of W. E. B. Du Bois: A Soliloquy on Viewing My Life from the Last Decade of Its First Century.* Edited by Herbert Aptheker. New York: International Publishers, 1968.

______. *The Correspondence of W. E. B. Du Bois.* Edited by Herbert Aptheker. 3 vols. Amherst: University of Massachusetts Press, 1973.

Eble, Kenneth E. *William Dean Howells.* Boston: Twayne, 1982.

______. *Old Clemens and W.D.H.: The Story of a Remarkable Friendship.* Baton Rouge: University of Louisiana Press, 1985.

Edel, Leon. *Henry James.* 5 vols. Philadelphia: J. B. Lippincott, 1953–1972.

Ellmann, Richard. *Oscar Wilde.* New York: Alfred A. Knopf, 1987.

Filler, Louis. *The Unknown Edwin Markham.* Yellow Springs, Ohio: Antioch Press, 1966.

Fine, Nathan. *Labor and Farmer Parties in the United States, 1828–1928.* New York: Rand School of Social Science, 1928; New York: Russell and Russell, 1961.

Foner, Philip S. *History of the Labor Movement in the United States.* 7 vols. New York: International Publishers, 1947–1965.

______. *Mark Twain, Social Critic.* New York: International Publishers, 1958.

______, ed. *The Autobiographies of the Haymarket Martyrs.* Introduction by William P. Black. New York: Humanities Press, for the American Institute for Marxist Studies, 1969; New York: Anchor Foundation, 1978.

———. *The Great Labor Upheaval of 1877.* New York: Monad Press, 1977.

Ford, Ford Madox. *Ford Madox Brown: A Record of His Life and Work.* London: Longmans, Green, 1896; New York: AMS Press, 1972.

Ford, Thomas W. "Howells and the American Negro." *Texas Studies in Language and Literature*, Vol. 5 (Winter 1964).

Freidel, Frank B. *The Splendid Little War.* Boston: Little, Brown, 1958.

Gayle, Addison. *Oak and Ivy: A Biography of Paul Laurence Dunbar.* Garden City, N.Y.: Doubleday, 1971.

Gibson, William M. "Mark Twain and Howells, Anti-Imperialists." *New England Quarterly*, Vol. 20 (December 1947).

Ginger, Ray. *The Bending Cross: A Biography of Eugene Victor Debs.* New Brunswick, N.J.: Rutgers University Press, 1949; New York: Russell and Russell, 1969.

———. *Altgeld's America: The Lincoln Ideal Versus Changing Realities.* New York: Funk and Wagnalls, 1958; New York: Franklin Watts–New Viewpoints, 1973; New York: Markus Wiener, 1986.

———. *Age of Excess: The United States from 1877 to 1914.* New York: Macmillan, 1965.

Goldman, Emma. *Living My Life: An Autobiography.* 2 vols. New York: Alfred A. Knopf, 1931; New York: Dover, 1970; Salt Lake City, Utah: G. M. Smith, 1982.

Gronlund, Laurence. *The Cooperative Commonwealth.* Boston: Lee and Shepard, 1884; Cambridge, Mass.: Belknap Press of Harvard University Press, 1965.

Gutman, Herbert G. "Workers Search for Power: Labor in the Gilded Age." In *The Gilded Age: A Symposium*, edited by Howard Morgan. Syracuse, N.Y.: Syracuse University Press, 1963.

Halfmann, Ulrich, ed. *Interviews with William Dean Howells.* Arlington: University of Texas Press, 1973.

Harlan, Louis. *Booker T. Washington: The Making of a Black Leader.* New York: Oxford University Press, 1972.

Harris, Frank. *The Bomb: A Novel.* New York: Mitchell Kennerley, 1909; Chicago: University of Chicago Press, 1963.

———. *Bernard Shaw.* New York: Simon and Schuster, 1931.

Heermance, J. Noel. *Charles W. Chesnutt, America's First Great Black Novelist.* Hamden, Conn.: Archon Books, 1974.

Hirsch, Eric L. *Urban Revolt: Ethnic Politics in the Nineteenth-Century Chicago Labor Movement.* Berkeley: University of California Press, 1990.

Holloway, Jean. *Edward Everett Hale: A Biography.* Austin: University of Texas Press, 1956.

———. *Hamlin Garland: A Biography.* Austin: University of Texas Press, 1960.

Hough, Robert L. *The Quiet Rebel: William Dean Howells as Social Commentator.* Lincoln: University of Nebraska Press, 1959.

Howells, Elinor Mead. *If Not Literature: Letters of Elinor Mead Howells.* Edited by Ginette Merrill and George Arms. Columbus: Ohio State University Press, 1988.

Howells, John Cooper. *Recollections of Life in Ohio from 1813 to 1840.* Introduction and conclusion by William Dean Howells. New introduction by Edwin H. Cady. Cincinnati, Ohio: Robert Clarke, 1895; Gainesville, Fla.: Scholars' Facsimiles and Reprints, 1963.

Howells, William Dean. *Life of Abraham Lincoln.* Columbus, Ohio: Follett, Foster, 1860; Bloomington: Indiana University Press, 1960.

———. *Life in Letters of William Dean Howells.* Edited by Mildred Howells. 2 vols. New York: Doubleday, Doran, 1928.

———. *Prefaces to Contemporaries, 1882–1920.* Edited by George Arms, William M. Gibson, and Frederic C. Marston, Jr. Gainesville, Fla.: Scholars' Facsimiles and Reprints, 1957.

———. *Letters of an Altrurian Traveler.* Edited by Clara M. Kirk and Rudolf Kirk. Gainesville, Fla.: Scholars' Facsimiles and Reprints, 1962.

———. *A Selected Edition of W. D. Howells.* General editor Edwin H. Cady. 32 vols. Bloomington: Indiana University Press, 1968–1991.

———. *William Dean Howells as Critic.* Edited by Edwin H. Cady. London: Routledge and Kegan Paul, 1973.

———. *Selected Letters of W. D. Howells.* Edited by Robert Cleitz, Richard H. Ballinger, and Christoph H. Lohmann. 6 vols. Boston: Twayne, 1980.

———. *Novels, 1875–1886: A Foregone Conclusion; A Modern Instance; Indian Summer; The Rise of Silas Lapham.* Edited by Edwin H. Cady. New York: Library of America, 1982.

———. *Novels, 1886–1888: The Minister's Charge; April Hopes; Annie Kilburn.* Edited by Don L. Cook. New York: Library of America, 1989.

Hudson, W. H. *A Crystal Age.* London: T. Fisher Unwin, 1887; New York: AMS Press, 1968; Folcroft, Pa.: Folcroft Library Editions, 1973.

Hughes, Langston. *Fight for Freedom: The Story of the NAACP.* New York: W. W. Norton, 1962.

Hulse, James W. *Revolutionists in London: A Study of Five Unorthodox Socialists.* Oxford: Clarendon Press, 1970.

Hunter, Robert. *Poverty.* New York: Macmillan, 1904; New York: Harper and Row, 1965.

———. *Socialists at Work.* New York: Macmillan, 1912.

———. *Violence and the Labor Movement.* New York: Macmillan, 1914; New York: Arno Press, 1969.

Jordan, P. D. "William Mackintire Salter." In *Dictionary of American Biography.* Vol. 16. Edited by Dumas Malone. New York: Scribners, 1936.

Josephson, Matthew. *Portrait of the Artist as American.* New York: Harcourt, Brace, 1930.

Kaplan, Justin. *Mr. Clemens and Mark Twain: A Biography.* New York: Simon and Schuster, 1966.

Kapp, Yvonne. *Eleanor Marx.* 2 vols. New York: Pantheon Books, 1977.

Kaufman, Stuart B. *Samuel Gompers and the Origins of the American Federation of Labor, 1848–1896.* Westport, Conn.: Greenwood Press, 1973.

Kebabian, John S., ed. *The Haymarket Affair and the Trial of the Chicago Anarchists, 1886: Original Manuscripts, Letters, Articles, and Printed Material of the Anarchists and of the State Prosecutor, Julius S. Grinnell.* New York: H. P. Kraus, 1970.

Kirk, Clara Marburg. *William Dean Howells, Traveler from Altruria, 1889–1894.* New Brunswick, N.J.: Rutgers University Press, 1962.

———. *William Dean Howells and Art in His Time.* New Brunswick, N.J.: Rutgers University Press, 1965.

Kirk, Clara Marburg, and Kirk, Rudolf. "Howells and the Church of the Carpenter." *New England Quarterly*, Vol. 32 (June 1959).

———. "Abraham Cahan and William Dean Howells: The Story of a Friendship." *American Jewish Historical Quarterly*, Vol. 52 (September 1962).

———. *William Dean Howells.* New York: Twayne, 1962.

———. "William Dean Howells, George William Curtis, and the Haymarket Affair." *American Literature*, Vol. 11, No. 4 (January 1969).

Larsen, Orvin P. *American Infidel: Robert G. Ingersoll.* New York: Citadel Press, 1962.

Lewis, R. W. B. *Edith Wharton: A Biography.* New York: Harper and Row, 1975.

Lidtke, Vernon *The Alternative Culture: Socialist Labor in Imperial Germany.* New York: Oxford University Press, 1985.

Lingeman, Richard R. *Theodore Dreiser.* 2 vols. New York: Putnam, 1986–1990.

Lloyd, Caro. *Henry Demarest Lloyd: A Biography, 1847–1903*. 2 vols. New York: Putnam, 1912.

Lovett, Robert Morss. *All Our Years: The Autobiography of Robert Morss Lovett.* New York: Viking Press, 1948.

Lum, Dyer D. *A Concise History of the Great Trial of the Chicago Anarchists.* Chicago: Socialistic Publishing Society, 1887; New York: Arno Press, 1969.

Lynn, Kenneth S. *William Dean Howells: An American Life.* New York: Harcourt Brace Jovanovich, 1971.

Lyon, David S. "The World of Peter J. McGuire: A Study of the American Labor Movement, 1870–1890." Ph.D. dissertation, University of Minnesota, 1972.

Mandel, Bernard. *Samuel Gompers: A Biography.* Yellow Springs, Ohio: Antioch Press, 1963.

Mann, Arthur. "Edwin D. Mead." In *Dictionary of American Biography.* Supp. 2. Edited by Robert Livingston Schuyler. New York: Scribners, 1958.

Marable, Manning. *W. E. B. Du Bois, Black Radical Democrat.* Boston: Twayne, 1986.

Marlatt, Gene R. "Joseph R. Buchanan, Spokesman for Labor During the Populist and Progressive Eras." Ph.D. dissertation, University of Colorado, 1975.

Marx, Eleanor, and Aveling, Edward. *The Working-Class Movement in America.* London: Swan, Sonnenschein, 1890; New York: Arno Press, 1969.

Marx, Eleanor; Lafargue, Laura Marx; and Longuet, Jenny Marx. *The Daughters of Karl Marx: Family Correspondence, 1866–1898.* Translated by Faith Evans. Notes and commentary by Olga Meier. Introduction by Sheila Rowbotham. New York: Harcourt, Brace, 1982.

Marx, Karl, and Engels, Frederick. *Letters to Americans, 1848–1895.* Translated by Leonard E. Mins. Edited by Alexander Trachtenberg. New York: International Publishers, 1953.

Matthiessen, F. O. *Sarah Orne Jewett.* Boston: Houghton Mifflin, 1929.

McKaye, Percy M. *Epoch: The Life of Steele McKaye.* New York: Boni and Liveright, 1927.

Meier, Paul. *William Morris, the Marxist Dreamer.* Translated by Frank Gubb. Preface by Robin Page Arnot. Sussex, England: Harvester Press, 1978; Atlantic Highlands, N.J.: Humanities Press, 1978.

Meltzer, Milton. *Mark Twain Himself: A Pictorial Biography.* New York: Thomas Y. Crowell, 1960.

———. *Bread and Roses: The Struggle of American Labor, 1865–1915.* New York: Alfred A. Knopf, 1967; New York: New American Library, 1977.

Minus, Paul M. *Walter Rauschenbusch, American Reformer.* New York: Macmillan, 1988.

Mordell, Albert. *Quaker Militant: John Greenleaf Whittier.* Boston: Houghton Mifflin, 1933.

Morgan, Austen. *James Connolly: A Political Biography.* Manchester, England: University of Manchester Press, 1988.

Morris, William. *News from Nowhere: An Epoch of Rest, Being Some Chapters from a Utopian Romance.* Boston: Roberts, 1891; New York: Penguin, 1984; London: Routledge and Kegan Paul, 1987.

———. *The Collected Letters of William Morris.* 2 vols. Edited by Norman Kelvin. Princeton, N.J.: Princeton University Press, 1987.

Myers, Gustavus. *History of the Great American Fortunes.* 3 vols. Chicago: Charles H. Kerr, 1907–1910; New York: Modern Library, 1936.

Nelson, Bruce. C. *Beyond the Martyrs: A Social History of Chicago's Anarchists, 1870–1900.* New Brunswick, N.J.: Rutgers University Press, 1988.

Nettles, Elsa. *Language, Race, and Social Class in Howells's America.* Lexington: University Press of Kentucky, 1988.

Olson, Robert. "Socialist and Realist: William Dean Howells." *Mainstream*, April 1, 1960.

Parsons, Lucy Eldine, ed. *The Accused and the Accusers: The Famous Speeches of the Eight Chicago Anarchists in Court.* Chicago: Socialistic Publishing Society, 1886, 1910; New York: Arno Press, 1969.

———. *The Life of Albert R. Parsons, with a Brief History of the Labor Movement in America.* Chicago: published by the author, 1889, 1903.

Peck, Harry Thurston. "William Dean Howells." In *The Personal Equation.* New York: Harper and Brothers, 1898.

Powderly, Terence V. *Thirty Years of Labor, 1859–1889.* Columbus, Ohio: Excelsior, 1890.

Pringle, Henry. *Theodore Roosevelt: A Biography.* New York: Harcourt, Brace, 1931.

Pugh, Patricia. *Educate, Agitate, Organise: One Hundred Years of Fabian Socialism.* London: Methuen, 1984.

Quint, Howard A. *The Forging of American Socialism: Origins of the Modern Movement.* Columbia: University of South Carolina Press, 1953.

Rampersad, Arnold. *The Art and Imagination of W. E. B. Du Bois.* Cambridge, Mass.: Harvard University Press, 1976; New York: Schocken Books, 1990.

Rauschenbusch, Walter. *Christianity and the Social Crisis.* New York: George H. Doran, 1907; New York: Harper and Row, 1964.

Reeve, Carl, and Reeve, Ann Barton. *James Connolly and the United States: The Road to the 1916 Irish Rebellion.* Atlantic Highlands, N.J.: Humanities Press, 1978.

Reichert, William O. *Partisans of Freedom: A Study in American Anarchism.* Bowling Green, Ohio: Bowling Green University Popular Press, 1976.

Roediger, David R., and Rosemont, Franklin. *Haymarket Scrapbook: A Centennial Anthology.* Chicago: Charles H. Kerr, 1986.

Roediger, David R., and Foner, Philip S. *Our Own Time: A History of American Labor and the Working Day.* New York: Greenwood Press, 1989.

Russell, Charles Edward. "Haymarket and Afterward: Some Personal Recollections." *Appleton's*, October 1907.

———. *Why I Am a Socialist.* New York: George H. Doran, 1910.

———. *These Shifting Scenes.* New York: George H. Doran, 1914.

Salvatore, Nick. *Eugene V. Debs, Citizen and Socialist.* Urbana: University of Illinois Press, 1982.

Schirmer, Daniel B. *Republic or Empire? American Resistance to the Philippine War.* Preface by Howard Zinn. Cambridge, Mass.: Schenkman, 1977.

Schuster, Eunice Minette. "Native American Anarchism: A Study of Left-Wing Individualism." *Smith College Studies in History*, Vol. 23, Nos. 1–4 (October 1931–July 1932).

Seretan, L. Glen. *Daniel De Leon: The Odyssey of an American Marxist.* Cambridge, Mass.: Harvard University Press, 1979.

Shaw, George Bernard; Besant, Annie; Bland, Hubert; Clarke, William; Olivier, Sydney; Wallas, Graham; and Webb, Sidney. *Fabian Essays in Socialism.* Edited by George Bernard Shaw. London: Fabian Society, 1889; Rutherford, N.J.: Fairleigh Dickinson University Press, 1984.

Smith, Greg, and Hyde, Sarah. *Walter Crane, Artist, Designer, and Socialist.* London: Lund Humphries, for the Whitworth Art Gallery, University of Manchester, 1989.

Spencer, Isobel. *Walter Crane.* New York: Macmillan, 1975.

Spies, August. *August Spies's Autobiography.* Chicago: Nina Van Zandt, 1887.

———. *Reminiszenzen.* Chicago: Christine Spies, 1888; New York: P. Lang, 1984.

Stallman, R. W. *Stephen Crane: A Biography.* New York: George Braziller, 1968.

Stidger, William L. *Edwin Markham.* New York: Abingdon Press, 1933.

Stone, Irving. *Clarence Darrow for the Defense: A Biography.* Garden City, N.Y.: Doubleday, Doran, 1941; New York: New American Library, 1971.

Stronks, James B. "Paul Laurence Dunbar and William Dean Howells." *Ohio Historical Quarterly*, Vol. 67 (1958).

Swanberg, W. A. *Dreiser*. New York: Scribners, 1965.

Swinton, John. *John Swinton's Paper*, 1883–1887. Tamiment Library, New York University.

Tarbell, Ida M. *All in the Day's Work: An Autobiography*. New York: Macmillan, 1939.

Taylor, Walter Fuller. "On the Origin of Howells's Interest in Economic Reform." *American Literature*, Vol. 2 (1930–1931).

———. *The Economic Novel in America*. Chapel Hill: University of North Carolina Press, 1942.

Tebbel, John. *An American Dynasty: The Story of the McCormicks, Medills, and Pattersons*. New York: Doubleday, 1947; New York: Greenwood Press, 1968.

Thomas, John L. *Alternative America: Henry George, Edward Bellamy, Henry Demarest Lloyd*. Cambridge, Mass.: Belknap Press of Harvard University Press, 1983.

Thompson, E. P. *William Morris, Romantic to Revolutionary*. New York: Pantheon Books, 1955, revised edition, 1977; Stanford, Calif.: Stanford University Press, 1988.

Tierney, Kevin. *Darrow: A Biography*. New York: Thomas Y. Crowell, 1979.

Tomalin, Ruth. *W. H. Hudson: A Biography*. London: Faber and Faber, 1982.

Tsuzuki, Chushichi. *The Life of Eleanor Marx, 1855–1898: A Socialist Tragedy*. Oxford: Clarendon Press, 1967.

Turaj, Frank. "The Social Gospel in Howells's Novels." *South Atlantic Quarterly*, Vol. 66 (Summer 1967).

Twain, Mark, and Howells, William Dean. *Mark Twain–Howells Letters*. Edited by Henry Nash Smith and William M. Gibson. Cambridge, Mass.: Belknap Press of Harvard University Press, 1960.

Vanderbilt, Kermit. *The Achievement of William Dean Howells: A Reinterpretation*. Princeton, N.J.: Princeton University Press, 1968.

Wagenknecht, Edward C. *William Dean Howells: The Friendly Eye*. New York: Oxford University Press, 1969.

Walker, Franklin D. *Frank Norris: A Biography*. New York: Russell and Russell, 1963.

Walsh, Harry. "Tolstoy and the Economic Novels of William Dean Howells." *Comparative Literature Studies*, Vol. 14 (June 1977).

Ward, John W. "Another Howells Anarchist Letter." *American Literature*, Vol. 22 (January 1951).

Weintraub, Stanley, ed. *Shaw: An Autobiography, Selected from His Writings*. 2 vols. New York: Weybright and Talley, 1969.

Wessinger, Catherine L. *Annie Besant and Progressive Messianism, 1877–1933*. Lewiston, N.Y.: E. Mellen Press, 1988.

Westbrook, Perry D. *Mary Wilkins Freeman*. Boston: Twayne, 1988.

White, Horace. *The Life of Lyman Trumbull*. Boston: Houghton Mifflin, 1913.

Whitlock, Brand. *Forty Years of It.* Introduction by William Allen White. New York: D. Appleton, 1914.

———. *The Letters and Journal of Brand Whitlock.* Edited by Allan Nevins. New York: D. Appleton–Century, 1936.

Whittier, John Greenleaf. *The Letters of John Greenleaf Whittier, 1861–1882.* Edited by John B. Pickard. 3 vols. Cambridge, Mass.: Belknap Press of Harvard University Press, 1975.

Wilson, A. N. *Tolstoy.* New York: W. W. Norton, 1988.

Wilson, Howard A. "William Dean Howells's Unpublished Letters About the Haymarket Affair." *Journal of the Illinois State Historical Society*, Vol. 56, No. 1 (Spring 1963).

Woodress, James L. *Booth Tarkington, Gentleman from Indiana.* Philadelphia: J. B. Lippincott, 1955; New York: Greenwood Press, 1969.

Wright, Conrad. "The Sources of Mr. Howells's Socialism." *Science and Society*, Vol. 2 (1938).

Wright, Robert G. *The Social Christian Novel.* New York: Greenwood Press, 1989.

Young, Art. *On My Way: Being the Book of Art Young in Text and Pictures.* New York: Horace Liveright, 1928.

———. *Art Young: His Life and Times.* Edited by John Nicholas Beffel. New York: Sheridan House, 1939.

Zeisler, Sigmund. *Reminiscences of the Anarchist Case.* Chicago: Literary Club of Chicago, 1927. Excerpted in *The Chicago Haymarket Riot: Anarchy on Trial*, edited by Bernard R. Kogan. Boston: D. C. Heath, 1959.

Index